Hooked

WHEN ADDICTION
HITS HOME

Edited by **CHLOE SHANTZ-HILKES**
with Decode

annick press
toronto + new york + vancouver

TO MY PARENTS. ALL OF THEM. —C. S.-H.

© 2013 Chloe Shantz-Hilkes (text)
Foreword © 2013 Marina Barnard
Introduction © 2013 Bob Munsch Enterprises Ltd.
Cover and interior design by Kong Njo
Cover image: © iStockphoto.com/anzeletti

Annick Press gratefully acknowledges the contribution of Decode, a global strategic consultancy firm that helps clients "decode" what young people think, feel, want, need, believe in, and aspire to.

Annick Press Ltd.

We acknowledge the support of the Canada Council for the Arts, the Ontario Arts Council, and the Government of Canada through the Canada Book Fund (CBF) for our publishing activities.

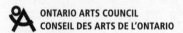

ONTARIO ARTS COUNCIL
CONSEIL DES ARTS DE L'ONTARIO

Cataloging in Publication

Hooked : when addiction hits home / edited by Chloe Shantz-Hilkes with Decode.

Issued also in electronic formats.
ISBN 978-1-55451-475-5 (bound).—ISBN 978-1-55451-474-8 (pbk.)

   1. Drug addicts—Family relationships—Canada—Juvenile literature.
2. Alcoholics—Family relationships—Canada—Juvenile literature.
3. Children of drug addicts—Canada—Juvenile literature. 4. Children of alcoholics—Canada—Juvenile literature. 5. Drug addiction—Psychological aspects—Juvenile literature. 6. Alcoholism—Psychological aspects—Juvenile literature. I. Shantz-Hilkes, Chloe II. DECODE (Firm)

HV5809.5.H65 2013   j362.29'13   C2012-907114-5

Distributed in Canada by:
Firefly Books Ltd.
66 Leek Crescent
Richmond Hill, ON
L4B 1H1

Published in the U.S.A. by:
Annick Press (U.S.) Ltd.
Distributed in the U.S.A. by:
Firefly Books (U.S.) Inc.
P.O. Box 1338, Ellicott Station
Buffalo, NY 14205

Printed in Canada

Visit us at: www.annickpress.com

MIX
Paper from
responsible sources
FSC® C004071

ANCIENT FOREST ™
FRIENDLY

Contents

Foreword

When we think of addiction we tend to think more about the person who suffers with it and less about those close to them who struggle in its undertow. Children whose parents are preoccupied with alcohol or drugs or gambling or even work, however, often have little choice but to try to find their place in an uncertain, topsy-turvy world spinning on an axis that revolves not around them, but around addiction. Children love their parents, frequently through thick and thin, and often when the parents are not worthy of that love. But it is hard to grow up always feeling second best to a parent's addiction.

So many of the young people whose stories animate these pages describe their disappointments, their confusion, their sadness and loss, their shame and anger. But they also talk about their love for and loyalty to their troubled parents, and their hopes for better days. This book addresses the more common types of addiction found in families, but its themes ring true for all dependency situations. While the drug or behavior of choice may vary, children's need for the attention and loving care of at least one parent or guardian does not.

The young people whose stories make up *Hooked* are remarkable in their willingness to tell stories often so private that they might not ever have shared them before, even with brothers or sisters. Their bravery in speaking out is a gift to the countless other children and young people out there who may draw comfort from realizing that they are not alone. This book may help them learn to name their conflicted feelings toward their parents through seeing that these are shared emotions and experiences.

These are, finally, hopeful stories. For even in recognizing the odds against them, these young people strive to make better lives for themselves and their families.

—Marina Barnard, Co-Director of the Centre for
Drug Misuse Research in Glasgow and author
of *Drug Addiction and Families* (JKP 2007).

Introduction

My addiction started with alcohol. I'm still not sure when I crossed the line, but eventually I was drinking in the mornings. My family knew something was wrong with me, but they didn't know what it was. My kids used to say, "Dad is weird. I talk to him and he doesn't answer. I talk to him and he isn't there."

After drinking for a long time, I went to Alcoholics Anonymous for help and I managed to stop. But it didn't last. Fifteen years later, I was visiting some friends who made their own wine, and I tried a glass. Six months after that, I was somewhere else and I had another glass. Before I knew it, I was drinking in earnest again. Eventually, I was also taking pain pills and crack cocaine. This time, addiction interfered with my life a lot more. I became unpredictable and sometimes behaved in ways I knew were destructive.

One day, I finally told my family how bad things had gotten. By that point, my children were adults and I had hidden my addiction for years. Their initial response was disbelief. They didn't want me to get help. They didn't want people to find out. But I eventually went to Narcotics Anonymous, and that's when I realized how much worse things could get.

I was one of the only people there who still had a family, a job, a house, and a car.

I'm sober now, but I'm not fixed. Using drugs for as long as I did messed up my ability to control myself. I was convinced I could do it just once more and then stop, but I couldn't. That's what makes addiction a disease, and that's the most important thing for the children of addicts to understand. My addiction was never my children's fault, and there was never anything they could do about it.

If your mom, or dad, or sibling, or aunt, or grandpa is an addict, you didn't cause their addiction and you can't cure it. If they make appointments with you and don't keep them, that's not your fault. If you talk to them and they don't listen, that's not your fault. If you have a family member who's an addict, that's not your fault.

I wish I had been open about my problems earlier and sought outside help for all of us—myself and my family. I also wish we had had family conversations about my situation. Staying away from drugs and alcohol and realizing that you can't "fix" or "cure" an addict may be the only way to ensure that you live your own life, and not theirs. But that doesn't mean you can't still love them. My own friends and family have been a tremendous source of support to me, and I wouldn't have made it through what I have without them.

—Robert Munsch, author of *The Paper Bag Princess*
and other beloved stories for children

Every Emotion Counts

Every Emotion Counts

Greg's father was an angry drunk. It took Greg a long time to realize that the best lesson his father's drinking taught him was to accept all his emotions, even when they seemed contradictory or wrong.

Dad's triggers

Most of the time when I was growing up, my father's alcoholism wasn't that noticeable. When he was sober, he was a really decent guy to be around. He always wanted to show us a good time. He'd take us skiing and camping and hiking. But he'd experienced a lot of nastiness and trauma as a kid, so there were certain things that would set him off, and that's when he would start drinking. Usually it was something to do with work. Sometimes it was a fight with Mom.

In many cases, alcoholism is not visible to most people. Alcoholics often seem normal to their colleagues and even friends. It is not uncommon for family to be the only ones who witness the effects that drinking has on an individual, particularly if he or she is a "functioning addict."

Once, when I was about eight, I was woken up in the middle of the night by the sounds of fighting. After things had finally died down a bit, I came into the living room to find that there were holes in the walls, and our TV was broken. My father had passed out on the sofa and my mom was in tears. After a while, she told me the reason Dad was so angry was because he couldn't watch a TV show he'd been looking forward to. We didn't get the channel, and so Dear Old Dad decided to go ballistic on the house. It was amazing. He really smashed the place up.

Another time, when I was ten, I woke up early in the morning to find our apartment full of smoke. Dad had fallen asleep drunk on the wicker sofa and his cigarette had ignited a cushion. My mother threw the cushion off the porch and onto the lawn. Somehow the furniture survived, but the house could easily have burned down if things had gone differently.

Dad gets arrested

The worst night of Dad's drinking for me came when I was in the eighth grade. I had broken my arm in gym class that afternoon so I had a cast on. My younger brother and I had both gone to bed, but our parents' fighting woke us up. They were screaming at each other, and throwing things; my father was incredibly drunk. My brother left and went to a friend's house, but I stayed.

I did my best to get between my mother and father—despite my broken arm—to prevent them from hurting each other. But no matter what I did, Dad wouldn't back down. At one point, my mother managed to get on the phone and had started telling a friend of hers what was going on when my dad ripped the phone right out of the wall. Fortunately, my mom's friend called the police.

Four cops arrived, tackled my father, and put him in handcuffs. I was terrified. My dad was a swimmer and a weight lifter, so he was really strong. At one point, three police officers were trying to get him in handcuffs and couldn't, so a fourth guy jumped on his back. Finally, my father just couldn't hold their collective weight. I'll never forget seeing his legs buckle. My dad could leg-press almost four hundred pounds, so it was terrible to see those muscular, athletic legs give out.

The rest of the time

There were also a lot of low-grade events where Dad would be intoxicated and nothing really major would happen. But even when things weren't over the top, it was impossible to have a relationship with someone who was completely hammered on gin most of the time.

You could tell immediately when Dad had been drinking. His facial expression was different and there was this nastiness that was just below the surface. You could tell by looking in his eyes: they were always sleepy and avoiding you. He wouldn't answer anything directly. And he would get really caught up in his own experience.

My reaction

Whenever Dad got drunk, I would immediately feel sadness, disappointment, frustration, and anger. It became so familiar—*here we go again*. But it was unpredictable too. Sometimes when he was drunk, the moment would pass without any danger. He would just fall asleep or something. But other times, all hell would break loose.

....

Many addicts behave differently each time they are under the influence. It is not unusual for alcoholics, in particular, to be affectionate sometimes and aggressive or depressed other times. This is because alcohol slows brain synapses and changes body chemistry, which can affect the drinker's mood in unpredictable ways.

....

Flirting with other women

The summer after the incident with the police, Dad and I had gone down to Cape Cod, just the two of us. By that point, my parents had basically announced they were splitting up, and my dad was still a young, attractive guy. While we were there, I discovered that he had a girlfriend. I was furious. I thought he should still be trying to make it work with Mom, and I knew he'd been with other women before. He taught at a college and he had affairs with at least three or four of his students.

One night, he came back to our room really drunk after hanging out with this girlfriend of his. I was fourteen at the time, and I pushed him up against the wall and told him I didn't want him to see her anymore. He flipped me around like it was nothing, held me up against the wall, and laughed. He said he "admired my spunk," but that I shouldn't try anything like that ever again. That's the way my dad was. There was just no messing with him, but I still tried a few times.

Fighting back

A few months after that trip, the whole family was back in Cape Cod together. That was right before my parents finally did split up, but we went on one last family trip first. One evening, we were watching TV and Dad was drunk, and I was really angry with him. So when he got up to rearrange the sofa that I was sitting on, I brought all my weight down so that its wooden leg landed directly on his foot. Right away I thought: *I can't believe I just did that!*

Dad was livid. He grabbed me and slammed me up against the window. My shoulders were on either side of the bar that ran down the middle of the glass, and I could feel the window moving in its frame, pressing outward. I knew that if I didn't escape he'd push me right through. I had this horrible mental image of getting all caught up in broken glass.

Somehow I broke free of his grip, jumped over the sofa, ran through the living room, and performed the single greatest athletic achievement of my life: I hurdled over the dining room table with all the chairs sitting around it. I think I managed it because I was just so scared that he was coming for me. I went through the back door and my mom and brother went through the front. God, it was so scary. We had no idea what he might do.

Fortunately, after we were out of the house, he didn't follow us. In fact, he calmed down really suddenly. Within minutes, we cautiously went back inside … and found him asleep. After all that, he had just gone upstairs to bed. It took me a lot longer than him to fall asleep that night.

How I coped

I developed a fairly constant depression while all this was going on. My days were colored by sadness and fear. On the one hand, I loved my dad a lot and looked up to him. After all, he was this really fun guy when he was sober. But on the other hand, he could be a terrifying drunk—so

I was often scared and angry too. And there was no one to explain to me that it made sense to feel the way I did.

I dealt with things—in part—by having a very active fantasy life. I dreamed about being able to swim fast, skate fast, and hold my breath underwater. I dreamed about having powers that helped me save my family from different villains. There was this never-ending supply of bad guys out there that I had to fight in superhuman ways. I think this allowed me to feel some sense of control over my own environment. I couldn't control the real world, so I controlled a fantasy world. It also helped me feel powerful, like I could make a difference.

My mother

Like my father, my mother was a trauma survivor. They both had abusive parents and had experienced a lot of violence when they were younger—so they were a perfect match in that sense. When my mom chose my dad, I think she unconsciously chose someone who would treat her the way she was treated by *her* father. Only what she didn't realize was that my dad was going to be way worse than hers.

My mother had gotten straight As while she was in school, but didn't have a college degree because she dropped out when she got pregnant with me. She came from a Roman Catholic family and gave birth to me only seven months after her marriage. Her mother would not talk to her for five years after I was born because she knew I'd been conceived before the wedding. So basically, my mom was flying solo.

She worked full-time, and spent the rest of her time thinking about how to keep us safe from her alcoholic husband. I think part of what was challenging for her was that we'd go through long periods where nothing bad happened. Then, suddenly, the wheels would fall off. The years I was thirteen and fourteen were the worst for that … and I guess that was all she could take.

Although she did leave my dad eventually, I remember my mother being very passive. I think that she was concerned for her own safety.

··

It can take many years for someone to leave an abusive relationship. In many cases, they never do. Sometimes this is because they fear they'd be unable to support themselves or their children without the abusive partner. Sometimes they are isolated, and don't know where to go. Sometimes (as with Greg's dad) the abuse is cyclical, and only occurs part of the time, making it hard to justify breaking up.

··

She worried that if she were to stand up to my father and tell him that his behavior was unacceptable, he would hurt her. So it wasn't until my father began having affairs that she finally said, "That's it. To hell with it."

Dad's departure

Immediately after my parents' divorce, Dad was living in a small apartment with my grandma and her new husband. It was tough to see that, because we'd always had a really comfortable living growing up. For most of my childhood my dad made quite a lot of money, so life after the divorce was quite the transition for him. Perhaps it's no surprise, then, that he soon decided to go teach in Ireland for a year. After that, he never seemed to want to live near us again. Almost as soon as he got back from Ireland, he took a position in Barbados and moved there for good.

In some ways, that was actually kind of cool. My brother and I went down to visit him when I was sixteen, and it was a neat place. He was still drinking, though, and never really got his act together. One night while we were there, he drank four-fifths of a bottle of rum. I remember getting up in the middle of the night to pour the remaining fifth down the drain.

Not long after we went home from that trip, we got a letter from one of his colleagues saying that he was in rough shape, and if somebody didn't come down to help him there was a good chance he would die. But by that time my family just didn't have the money for anyone to fly there. He was on his own.

Getting the news

We found out my father had died because Mom got a letter from the university where he was working. It said that the coroner's report had revealed a foreign substance in his blood. So we think that he overdosed—accidentally or maybe on purpose. My mother burst into tears when she told me about the letter. I hugged her and said, "Well, we kind of knew it was coming."

Later that night, I went into town and hung out with a friend of mine and walked around. It was the strangest experience because, despite the fact that his death wasn't a surprise, I still felt so stunned.

Looking back

My biggest regret about growing up with my dad is that I lost so many opportunities. Most of all, I lost the opportunity to feel like I was a lovable human being. For the longest time I felt as if nobody had any reason to like me. I'm married now, with kids, but I didn't have any enduring relationships until I was in my thirties. I was always really clumsy, really goofy, and really shy.

I also lost the opportunity to do well in school, because I was constantly fighting sadness or anger or depression.

My father was always worried about something, and so I worried too. I spent so much time worrying that I found it hard to make friends or do well academically. I worried about things at home and, above all, about my conflicting emotions.

That's why my advice to anyone going through something like this is to pay attention to *every* emotion. If you sometimes feel like you hate your parent and sometimes feel like you love him or her, that's okay. Both feelings can be true. I always used to wonder if one of my feelings was wrong. But now I know that you've got to accept all your emotions, even if they seem to totally contradict each other. It took me a long time to figure that out. Now that I finally have, it's a weight off my shoulders.

Learning to Forgive
Learning to Forgive

Jenny was the glue that held her family together while her mom's gambling was tearing it apart. She dealt with the stress by forgiving her mom—over and over and over again.

Finding out

My family didn't have a lot of money when I was growing up. We were immigrants and my parents both worked really hard to make ends meet. Before my brother was born, I was alone a lot of the time because my parents were both so busy at their jobs. So when one of my mom's friends first told me that she had lost $3,000 gambling, I couldn't believe it! My mom was always a huge penny-pincher, and was really strict about money, so I thought, *There's no way she would throw that kind of money away.*

Like all addictions, gambling addiction is not rational. Compulsive gamblers can't control their impulse to chase bets, even if they are otherwise logical people and know their behavior is hurting their families. They will continue to gamble, despite losing routinely. Therapy, group support, and other techniques can help problem gamblers overcome their addiction.

I don't know how much my mom ultimately lost—or won. But I assume she lost because you never win against the house, and we never seemed to have a lot of money. And my mom never hesitated to remind us how hard she had to work so that we could afford everything. So her gambling just seemed like such a contradiction to all the things she always told me about being responsible. And for a long time, I was in denial about her addiction.

Hard to believe

Part of the reason for my disbelief was probably the fact that I never really saw my mom gambling. My family is Vietnamese, and in our culture a lot of people gamble casually for fun, but my parents never really did that in our home. Instead, my mom would go away to the casino for long periods of time. Also, no one in my family really talked about my mom's gambling problem, so I mostly just heard about it from other people. My mom's friends would make comments about her losing money, but I wasn't sure what to believe. No one wants to think badly of his or her parents, so I was really reluctant to admit that my mom had a problem. I felt so betrayed, because it went against everything she was always saying to me. Finding out about that $3,000 loss when I was fourteen was definitely one of those moments when you realize that your parents aren't perfect, that their actions aren't always right.

Long absences

Even after I became aware of my mom's gambling, I kind of brushed it off. But gradually it became too bad to ignore. By the time I was in my late teens, my mom had started disappearing to the casino for days on end.

Sometimes she'd only be gone for a day, but others she'd be gone over the weekend, if not longer. She never called to check in or let us know when she was gone. I used to worry that something might have happened to her, and that I wouldn't be able to tell if it did. So there was always that fear—that she might be in trouble, or that she was never going to come back. There were times I thought I should call the police, but I didn't know what I'd say if I did.

Dad's anger was deflected onto me

My mom's absences created a lot of tension between my parents, and my dad began to make really angry remarks about my mom. He would say to me, "Oh, she's out gambling again. She's so irresponsible." And because my mom was never around when my dad was most angry with her, he would deflect that anger onto me. Funnily enough, I think it was my dad's rants that made me angriest toward my mom, not so much because of what she was doing, but because she was making my dad say mean things about her. I ended up being mad at both my parents a lot because they put me in this position.

Trying to make amends

Whenever my mom was away for days at a time gambling, she would always come back from the casino with food for my brother and me. She would present us each with takeout containers of fried chicken or Chinese. I don't know why, but we always accepted them gratefully. I think she meant for the food to be like a peace offering—a way to get us to forgive her for the long absence. And even though it was totally inadequate, we were always so glad to have her back that we would take it and eat it. It was a ritual; it was her way of getting us to talk to her again.

Keeping the family together

In the midst of all this, I felt like the glue that was holding my family together. My parents never talked to each other, and my brother was too young for either of them to talk to, so I was the link between everybody. It felt as though if I weren't there, the family would break apart. Meanwhile, all my friends were dealing with different things—they were busy worrying about boys or shopping for new clothes—and there I was, trying to keep my family intact.

One time, when my mom had disappeared for a few days to go gamble, I stayed late at school to finish a group project. And I guess I had forgotten to tell my dad that I was going to be home later than normal, because he got really scared and sent some of my friends to look for me.

Finally, one of them found me in the library and said, "Come quick. Your dad is really worried about you. He called me because he thought that your mom had kidnapped you." When my dad picked me up, he was so emotional. I remember we were in the car and he was crying. I don't think I had ever seen him cry before then. That's when he told me he was afraid he was going to lose one of us. I think he was scared that my mom would either drive me away with her gambling or would take me away herself. And if I were gone, he wouldn't have anyone to confide in.

How I coped

The funny thing is, even though I was angry a lot of the time, my parents would tell you that I was a really good kid. And it's true. I was always very obedient. I was the kind of kid that makes adults say, "You should be more like Jenny." Instead of confronting my mom about her gambling or telling my dad to stop ranting to me, I took my frustrations out online. I had a website and I would spend hours and hours writing about my life there. I liked it because it was totally anonymous. I didn't know any of the people who were reading it and they didn't know me. My mom was a very private person, and I think that's one of the things that I inherited from her. I've never enjoyed talking about my problems with friends, and it's always been easier for me to talk to strangers. So I would write about how I felt toward my parents and about the things they did to me. Anyone visiting my site read a lot of angry posts.

For the most part, that's what I did instead of getting angry with my parents. But there was also a brief time when I became more rebellious and started to talk back. I remember once, my dad was lecturing me about doing well in school and I said to him, "Dad, I'll do well in school, and I'll get a good job, but it won't be because of you."

Mom was off limits

Although I would sometimes get angry with my dad, I never confronted or talked back to my mom. My dad was usually an easygoing guy, but my mom was a lot more intense. I think I was afraid that if I ever pushed her too hard, she would go away and just disappear forever. I remember one time when I was about fourteen and my mom was really angry with my dad. I don't remember why, but she said to me, "What do you think your dad would do if we all died? Do you think he would feel guilty?" Obviously, that's a pretty scary thing to hear, so I was always afraid that if I confronted my mom about her gambling, she would do something unexpected or extreme.

My brother, my comforter

Aside from writing, something that comforted me while all of this was going on was my brother. He was always very attached to me, and I really appreciated having him around. We're very different in a lot of ways. I'm a lot like my parents—I'm not very affectionate, and I don't always find it easy to talk to people—but my brother is the opposite. Unlike me, he was born and raised in Western society, and I think people here tend to be more warm and communicative. When our parents were fighting, or my mom was away, he would often say to me, "Can't you do something about this?" or "Doesn't this bother you?" I usually couldn't respond. Most of the time I would tell him, "Just ignore it." Even though I didn't always know how to help him, knowing there was someone else in the same situation as me made me feel better. And I did my best to make life special for him. Our parents didn't celebrate Christmas, but I always made sure that he got a Christmas present or two from me.

Learning to forgive

The thing that helped me most of all was learning to forgive my parents. It sounds like a cliché, I know, but it's true. And it wasn't something I just did one time; it's something I had to do over and over again. Every time my mom was away for days at a time, I forced myself to forgive her. And every time my dad got mad at her for gambling and took it out on me, I forgave him. It was really hard to do, but that process of forgiving them was really powerful for me. I don't think it would help everyone, but it has definitely helped me. And I think I was able to do it partly because I knew it could always be worse. I knew that other people's moms went away and never came back, but mine always did.

A Tough Road

A Tough Road

Jermaine was always fending for himself and dealing with his crack-cocaine-addicted dad's paranoia and abuse. He finally learned that sometimes you have to turn your back on your parents.

My dad, the addict

I first found out that my dad was addicted to crack cocaine because he told me. He didn't tell my mom, he didn't tell anyone else, he told me. At the time, I was only seven or eight. I didn't cry or anything, but it was definitely a big burden for him to tell me alone. And it got worse. Shortly after he told me, he went through a period where every couple of weeks he would get so high smoking crack that he'd say to me, "I'm going to die. You have to get me ready to go to the hospital. I'm going to die."

....

Feelings of anxiety and paranoia are a common side effect of cocaine consumption. Sometimes cocaine even causes hallucinations that can make the user feel he or she is about to die.

....

Later, I found out that the cocaine was making him paranoid, but at the time I didn't know that. So I would put him in clothes and wipe him up because he'd throw up on himself sometimes, but by the time we'd be ready to go, he'd no longer be as high, so he'd decide we didn't have to. That was very draining. Not long after that, he'd usually be back in the bathroom getting high again. That's where he always did cocaine. After a while, it got to a point where I sometimes hoped he would die. I went from hoping he'd stay alive to hoping he'd die very quickly.

No one noticed

For quite a while my dad had a good-paying job at a factory, and we were never poor or anything. But he took tons of time off and stayed home a lot to take drugs. That usually meant I stayed home to look after him. And none of my teachers ever caught on. I was really good at acting like nothing was wrong, so most of them just assumed I was skipping class, I guess. But in reality, my mom would be at work and I'd be at home with my dad and my sister.

My mom worked at a call center and was usually gone from six in the morning until six in the afternoon. That really sucked because it meant that she left the house before I had the chance to. So because of that, I got stuck at home with dad instead of her. Even after she got off work, my mom would often go get massages or get her hair done before coming home. That was even worse than her leaving early, because like I said, my dad got really paranoid when he was high. That meant he didn't like to have lights on in the house because he thought people could see in. So we would sometimes spend hours sitting around in the dark, waiting for my mom to come home and turn some lights on. That was terrifying—especially in the winter when it got dark early.

Protecting Caitlin

To make matters worse, I'd have to watch my little sister too. I have three sisters now, but this was when I was only eight and I just had one. Caitlin was just two years old while most of this was going on, and I would sit in the hallway between our living room (where she was playing) and the bathroom (where my dad was doing cocaine) and try to keep an eye on both of them.

Sometimes I feel like I've spent my whole life doing my best to protect Caitlin from my dad's drug use, since my mom wouldn't. A lot of the time I was so desperate just to keep her out of the bathroom and away from my dad that I would act like her slave. I would get her anything she asked for, just to keep her from going near my dad while he was using. Now that we're older, I sometimes feel like she still expects me to run around and get everything for her, because that's what she became used to.

My mom, the denier

Meanwhile, my mom never said anything about my dad taking drugs. Like I said, she was out of the house most of the time, and when she *was* around, she was in total denial about my dad's addiction. She would spend hours looking through medical books to try to figure out why he was "sick." Even I, as a little kid, *I* knew something was wrong, but my mom didn't want to acknowledge that one little bit. My dad even told me that he sometimes tried to make her realize that he was in trouble, that he needed help. He said one time she came into the bathroom while he was getting high and he didn't even try to hide it. Instead, he blew a big cloud of crack cocaine smoke right in her face. But she just pretended it never happened.

••

It is not uncommon for addicts to go through periods where they stop making any efforts to hide their behavior. This is sometimes a cry for help, and sometimes a form of manipulation—a way of demonstrating that they are in control and there's nothing anyone can do to stop them from abusing their substance of choice.

••

Sleepless nights

When I was a little bit older, my mom went from working the day shift to working nights. At that point, my parents weren't sleeping in the same room because they went to bed at totally different times. And since my dad couldn't sleep with my mom, he would sleep on the top bunk of my bunk bed, which was normally empty. He wouldn't really sleep, though, because he was so paranoid. And to make matters worse, he wouldn't let me sleep either. In fact, he would sometimes punch me awake at night because he was scared of drifting off and not waking up. After a while, it didn't even hurt when he hit me because I was just so tired. Mostly it annoyed me, because sometimes I would *just* have fallen asleep and then he'd wake me. Ever since then, I've been a bit of an insomniac.

One of the most annoying times he did this was on my tenth birthday. I was sleeping on the couch in the living room and my dad came and sat on me for two hours. It sounds weird, I know, but he literally came and sat on top of me. And I remember exactly how long he sat on me because I was watching the clock the whole time, thinking, *This can't last much longer.* But it did. He was just ranting, and complaining, and cussing, and talking. Eventually he stood up and actually yelled at me for not telling him to get off me earlier, but it just hadn't occurred to me to do so. See, I was always very obedient. Even when I was just one or two years old, if you told me to sit still, I would literally sit still until you told me I could move again—sometimes for hours. So I just lay there, assuming he was going to get up eventually. I don't know why I was so obedient. I was a really smart kid too, so I think maybe I realized that if you did what people told you to, it would save you a lot of time and trouble. But sometimes it also meant that your dad sat on you for two hours when he was stoned.

Blaming me

It's always been really hard for me to ask for stuff that I want. Even when I was a really little kid, I never asked my mom for gifts or anything. I worried she'd say no, or feel like she had to say yes. My sister, on the other hand, has to have everything she wants. Ironically, that's one of my dad's biggest complaints about me. He says I should ask for things more—like Caitlin does. He actually told me once that he loves her more because she asks him for the things she wants and stands up for herself more than I do. He's even gotten mad at me a couple of times for not asking him to stop taking drugs! He says, "If you told me to stop, then I'd stop."

Many addicts try to blame others—most often family members—for their behavior. This can help them justify their continued abuse, and it can alleviate their guilt by placing some of the responsibility on people who are, in fact, victims.

Once, he asked me to bring him his shoes. And I knew that he kept his stash in his shoes, but I did what I was told. Then he yelled at me for being "an enabler."

••

An enabler *is someone who intentionally or unintentionally does something that makes it easier for his or her loved one to continue engaging in destructive behavior. In some cases, enabling can contribute to ongoing substance abuse.*

••

But of course, he would have gotten mad at me if I *hadn't* brought the shoes too. So I couldn't win. He would also tell me that I should hate him. He'd say, "You hate me, don't you? You hate me, don't you?" And I'd say no. Once, after I said no, he spat on me. It was like he was trying to make me hate him ... or wanted me to.

How I coped

Even before I learned about my dad's addiction, I was a weird kid. I remember this one time when I was just four years old and a friend of mine asked me to go on the seesaw with him. And I said no, because in my head I thought: *We're going to go on the seesaw, and you're going to want to go faster. I'm going to fall off and crack my head open, and my parents are going to be sad when I die.* I'm weird like that. I worry about things and analyze things before they've happened. But I think maybe that was one of the ways I learned to deal with things, by planning for them and expecting the worst.

Another thing that helped was to get out of the house. On days that I actually made it to school, I would always try to avoid coming home. If I ever had to go back for lunch money or something like that, I would try to get someone to hand it to me through the kitchen window. I knew that if I actually went inside, I'd somehow get roped into staying there. When that didn't work and I was forced to come inside, I would just do my best to zone everything out. I guess that was my main way of coping. Every once in a while I couldn't ignore things, though. And one time in particular, I lost it.

Kicking Dad out

By this point I was about sixteen years old, and I had two sisters, Caitlin and Kim. My dad had gotten really stoned one night and was so paranoid that he actually kicked us out of the house. We went to the mall, because my mom was at work. I must have called her a hundred times, but she never picked up. Later, she had the nerve to get mad at me for calling so much, so that made me even angrier. Finally, she came home and convinced my dad to open the door and we all went back inside. After that, they were in the living room arguing and I finally just couldn't take it anymore. I walked into the room and I said to my dad, "You have to leave. You're always calling me a wuss and telling me I should stand up to you. Well, now I am. Get out." Amazingly, he left.

He was back around three in the morning, though.

"I need to use the bathroom," he said.

I wasn't buying it. "There's a Tim Hortons up the road. Use the bathroom there."

"I have to get some stuff."

"Come get it in the morning."

"I need my wallet."

"I'll get you your wallet and then you can go."

Finally, he left and my mom thanked me for dealing with him. I guess I appreciate her saying thank you, but at the same time, that should never have been my job; it should have been hers. There's no point trying to confront my mom about anything, though. If I told my mom, "You should have come home earlier" or "You should have returned my calls," I knew she'd say, "I needed time for myself" or "I had a long day." And meanwhile I'd be stuck at home watching my sisters and trying to convince my dad he wasn't going to die.

Dad was back in the house again not long after that. He was only supposed to visit during the day, but he started sleeping in his car outside the house. So finally my mom took pity on him and started letting him sleep inside again. She actually asked my permission. And I was like, "Sure. Whatever." I found it hard to say no to her, and I didn't know where else he would go, but I didn't like it.

After that, he relapsed again and things were basically back to the way they were before, except something had changed for me. I'd had enough. I left as soon as I could after that.

Looking back

Once, when I was in high school, we watched a movie about drug addicts. And what really got me was that so many of them were people who started using despite the fact that they were really smart and had really good jobs. One of the girls in the movie had a job in the White House. One of the guys used to be a really successful businessman who now sneaks into hotels for the free breakfasts. It made me think about how, at one point, my dad probably had so much potential but wasted it on drugs.

The good news is he's stopped doing coke now. He went to rehab and had one relapse afterward, but that was it. It's funny, because he doesn't have a sponsor or anything, but he seems to be doing okay. My three sisters still live at home, so I'm glad he won't put them through the same awful stuff he put me through. It's still hard for me to go home, though, partly *because* things aren't as bad anymore, so my sisters have a hard time understanding why I had to leave.

It's been a tough road for me. Because of everything I went through with my dad, I've been on antipsychotics and antidepressants for a long time now, and they make you kind of numb. I also have obsessive-compulsive disorder, which makes me really anxious, and can get me fixated on certain things. I've been on drugs for that as well, but lately I've been trying to avoid all those medications because they remind me too much of my dad.

I'm actually living with my girlfriend now, and we recently had a baby. I can only hope that I do a better job of being a dad than my dad did. I'm pretty sure I will, because I spent so much of my childhood taking care of everyone else in my family.

Nothing to Do with Me

Nothing to Do with Me

Hannah's father often embarrassed her with his overeating and public drunkenness. But growing up she knew that she was normal, and solid, and sane—and that his bad behavior wasn't her fault.

Two different dads

When I was just four or five years old, I asked my mom, "What's wrong with Dad?" He seemed to me to be two different people in one body—as if he had two personalities when everybody else I knew only had one. I think the fact that I picked up on that when I was so young says a lot.

••

Drinking can often lead to personality and behavioral changes. Someone who is normally friendly can become angry and aggressive after a few drinks. Other drinkers become depressed, while still others become unnaturally happy and euphoric. Researchers believe this is because alcohol prevents the brain from functioning normally.

••

When my dad *wasn't* drinking, he was generous, caring, funny, and charismatic: a loving person with a good heart. When he *was* drinking, his personality would completely morph. It was like Jekyll and Hyde. This other person—the drunk one—would often say things that were inappropriate, obnoxious, lewd, and offensive. Sometimes, he would sit at the kitchen table and after a few glasses of scotch or wine, he would sort of slump forward and his eyes would droop and he would get all deep, brooding, and philosophical—always in a negative way. He seemed to have a lot of stress in his life. Something was dogging him and he was trying to escape it, or to cope with it internally. I'm not sure I will ever know what it was. After a while, it got so my little sister, Emma, and I would see it coming and we'd roll our eyes and think, *Here we go again.*

Drunk Dad was angrier than normal Dad too. Once, when I was nine, he got really mad at me. We had a refrigerator with two handles, one for the fridge and one for the freezer. Well, I decided he'd had enough to drink so I took my bicycle lock and locked the two handles together so he couldn't get at the wine. After I did it, I went outside to get away from him. Of course, shortly afterward, my mom came looking for me because Dad was "not happy." She wasn't kidding. When I got home, he was furious, and shouting … really, really angry. His drunkenness would often make him angry like that, and in between bouts of being angry he would drink, and eat; and drink, and eat; and drink.

Embarrassed by Dad

Because of his overconsumption of alcohol and food, there was one phrase that my dad heard me say often: "Dad, you're embarrassing me!" And it was true. I tried to ignore it most of the time, but when I couldn't ignore it, I simply felt ashamed. He would pass out on the couch while my friends were over. And there were a few times when he actually threw up in public.

Once, my whole family was out to dinner at a nice restaurant and he ate and drank so much that he threw up right at the table. Then, as we were leaving, he threw up again in the parking lot, and the restaurant staff had to hose down the pavement. He kept stumbling around and making a scene. I usually did my best not to take things too seriously, but I sure wasn't laughing then. I remember sitting silently in the backseat with my sister while my mom drove us all home. We were just so mortified that no one said anything.

My mom, the middlewoman

Maybe I idealize my mother or have a tendency to look at her with rose-colored glasses, but honestly, I think she did a really good job of getting in between my dad and me. She did her best to calm him down, but also recognized that I was less than thrilled with the situation. She obviously knew that it wasn't ideal for a child to be sitting at a kitchen table with a father so drunk that his eyes were glazed over. So she always had to walk that line between the two of us, especially because I would sometimes bait my dad and provoke him. So my mom was always doing her best to persuade me to go outside and play rather than irritate Dad.

While I was growing up, my dad always worked and my mom stayed home. That was their deal. I think part of the reason that suited my mom was because, with Dad away so much, she could kind of do her own thing. So, despite his behavior, she was able to have some sense of normalcy, and a routine, and a nice house. Sometimes it felt like our real family consisted of my mom, my little sister, and me. And as soon as Dad came home it felt like we were walking on eggshells—not knowing what his mood would be.

I'm not sure what made my mom stay with my dad for so long. Eventually he left her for another woman, but I don't think my mom ever dreamed of leaving him. You have to be a certain kind of person to say, "I'm not putting up with this." My mom wasn't that kind of person.

How I coped

Sometimes I would try to call my dad out when he had been drinking and was acting like a jerk. Later, I realized that you can't really have a logical conversation with someone when they're drunk like that.

Talking to an alcoholic while he or she is drunk is inevitably very frustrating and unproductive. It's virtually impossible to win an argument with a drunk person, and even if you do manage to have a worthwhile conversation, they may not remember it properly the next day.

He'd be slurring his words, and I would make jokes about it to try to get him to realize how ridiculous he sounded. I took comfort in the humor. Something he could never pronounce properly when he was drunk was "key lime pie," and to this day I only have to say those three words to my sister and we'll both burst out laughing.

As I got older and became more moody, I began to have less and less patience for my dad's behavior. Gradually I entered a really rebellious phase, where I began to clash with my dad even more. After a while, I was doing more than just making jokes about his behavior; I was actually saying to him, "This isn't cool. You can't behave this way. What do you think you're doing?" By the time I was in my teens, I had started to think of his habits as unacceptable rather than just funny and sad.

Not my problem

I think what saved me from becoming too upset about my dad was the fact that I always knew I had nothing to do with his bad behavior. That's huge. I think if you know that what somebody is doing is simply not okay, then you're not as much of a victim. I obviously wished my dad were different. I saw other kids who had nice relationships with their dads and I thought: *Wouldn't it be nice to have a dad like that? Wouldn't it be nice to have a dad who was interested in me, and what I'm going through?* But I didn't spend a lot of time in my room crying about it, because I think that's where suffering comes in. I was more like: *Well, this is a less than ideal situation ... but I guess* c'est la vie.

I think it would have been hard for me to have a sense of humor about my dad if it weren't for my mom. She did a pretty good job of being the mediator in our family, and she raised my sister and me to be solid people. It's hard not to take things personally unless you feel good about yourself and are okay in your own skin. And I think I owe that to my mom, because she helped me establish what normal was; and I knew I was okay, and normal, and sane.

Losing all control

I think all the drinking numbed my dad to normal feelings and sensations. That would explain why he never realized that he was eating too much. He just never seems to feel full. You or I would eat a turkey dinner and say, "I'm stuffed," but you'll never hear my dad say that. If he's enjoying the taste of something, he'll keep putting it on his plate until his body simply cannot handle any more food. He eventually throws up, because that's his body's only way to make him stop eating.

Eating and drinking aren't the only ways my dad overindulges, either. Whether it's food, alcohol, or sex, he just wants, wants, wants. He doesn't have the normal reflexes that the rest of us have that make us stop doing something when we've had enough of it. Instead, he keeps going until he's passed out, or throwing up, or his relationships are damaged.

The affair

When I was ten, I had a dream one night that there was a woman hiding in the bathroom of our house and that my mom found her. I woke up sweating and crying, and I guess I must've known that something was going on with my dad. My mom later told us that he was cheating on her—and not for the first time. Like with food and alcohol, he couldn't stop himself from being unfaithful. And as I said, he eventually left my mom for another woman, and that was the point when I just couldn't put up with it anymore. My mom had been tolerating him all these years, and then he leaves her? It was so not okay. I remember swearing at him and telling him I thought he was a liar and a cheater and a jerk. That was another one of those times when, try as I might, I couldn't find anything to laugh about.

Moving on

To this day, my dad hasn't really changed. I still love him and we still spend time together. He takes more of an interest in my life now that I am an adult and he can relate to me, but I've come to accept the fact that he will probably never get better. I now believe that you cannot really expect people to change in the long run, but you can definitely learn from your experiences with them. Because of what I've gone through with my dad, I don't drink, smoke, or do drugs. Neither does my sister. That's not a bad thing.

I also learned a lot growing up with my dad. I learned to work hard and be independent. That's meant that I've always taken my job really seriously and done well at it. And I learned that extremes are dangerous. My dad was so prone to extremes that I quickly realized how desire can become destructive. Living with someone like him helped me understand what balance looks like. It helped me understand the kind of person I wanted to be ... and the qualities I wanted to cultivate. I learned that you can burn energy wishing things would change (and they might not), or you can focus on the positive and make the most of your circumstances.

Everything is temporary. One day you will move on and create the life you want for yourself. In the meantime, if it is hard to watch someone behave the way they do, keep in mind that it probably has nothing to do with you at all.

No Reason to Be Ashamed

No Reason to Be Ashamed

No one in Pierre's family
ever acknowledged his
mother's alcoholism.
And for a long time,
the secrecy and mistrust
prevented Pierre from
speaking about anything—
including the fact that
he was gay.

Surrounded by drinking

My mother is American, but my twin brother, Remy, and I grew up in France, where my father is from. We lived there until I was fifteen and my parents divorced. During our time in France, my mother drank pretty steadily. There was this whole community of mothers who stayed home during the day and drank together. My friend Thérèse's mother was also an English-speaker, and an alcoholic. Our two families formed a unit where the drinking started early, with cocktails around eleven a.m., and ended in the evening after dinner. It was a way of life growing up, and my mother certainly wasn't the only one who did it.

How it affected her

My mother's drunkenness became most apparent in the evenings. Her speech would slur and her emotional state would change. Aside from telling us she loved us, my mother was emotionally guarded when she was sober. When she was drunk, her guard would slip. Sometimes she would become affectionate; sometimes she would become mean. If my father was away, she would often have breakdowns and cry. She was not what you would call a happy drunk. All the emotional baggage she managed to evade during the day would sort of catch up with her in the evening after she'd been drinking.

I remember asking my mother when I was quite young why she was so different at night, but I don't think I actually used the word "alcoholic" until I was thirteen or so. Around that time, Thérèse and I both came to the conclusion that our mothers were alcoholics, and we'd compare notes about their drinking habits. We'd say, "Your mother is a better drunk driver than mine is," or "Your mother is a nicer drunk than mine."

My mother and Thérèse's mother had a pretty toxic relationship. They were very competitive—partly because they were both in love with my father. Much later, after my parents had split up, my dad and Thérèse's mom ended up together. Long before that, though, our moms used to compare lives and try to one-up each other. And because my mother was so crippled by insecurities and felt like such a failure, she could never win.

Once, after one of these "whose life is better" sessions, Remy and I came home to find our mother in the bathroom crying, saying how her life was worthless and meaningless. We tried to console her as best we could, but we were only ten and we didn't really understand where this was coming from.

Failed by her kids

Sometimes my mother's emotional outbursts had to do with our performance in school. My mother had a very high IQ and held us to high academic standards. But because she was usually drunk in the evenings, she never provided us with much guidance or support.

I remember one semester—around the time that our parents' marriage was first on the rocks—during which Remy and I were not getting good grades. When we brought our report cards home, my mother went into this rage. She said things like: "I've sacrificed my life for you, and this is how you repay me? My life is worthless! I should just throw myself off the balcony." It went on and on and on, all because we hadn't reached the level of academic success that she expected of us. That really struck the fear of God in us.

When I look back now, I'm pretty sure my mother was never suicidal. Despite the occasional threat, I don't think she ever really considered killing herself. But at the time, we took it as literal truth that we were both terrible failures, that we had let her down so badly that she might do something awful. I felt like I would lose my mother because I hadn't worked hard enough. I felt like my Cs were the reason she was sad. And so I redoubled my efforts, and so did Remy, and we both rose to the top of our class.

Dad didn't help

Although my father wasn't an alcoholic, he *did* drink, and he was certainly very tolerant of my mother's drinking. In fact, he has told me that from the time they first began dating, he knew she was an alcoholic. Despite this, he never discussed her drinking with her.

Instead, he was usually the first to pour her another glass. My father comes from a drinking culture, so his relationship with alcohol is very different from my mother's. In France, most people drink with every meal except breakfast. So I think that contributed to my father's tolerance of my mother's drinking. And despite the fact that it was way beyond normal, nobody spoke about—or even acknowledged—my mother's drinking.

....

Avoidance and denial are very common problems in the families of addicts. Many addicts' partners and spouses will sometimes go so far as to facilitate ongoing substance abuse, rather than risk confronting or shaming their loved one.

....

After the divorce

Our parents got divorced when Remy and I were fifteen, and Mom's drinking went from bad to worse. She had signed a prenuptial agreement with my father, which left her with very little. As a result, we were forced to move back in with her family in the United States. My mother's father, also an alcoholic, had passed away years before, and none of her remaining family members drank. This meant that on top of becoming more frequent, my mother's drinking also became more noticeable.

I can't remember a time after we moved back to the States that my mother was coherent beyond seven or eight p.m. On weekends it was even worse: by four p.m. she'd be slurring her speech and passing out on the sofa. That was something we hadn't really witnessed in France. Sunday afternoons in France were spent with my father's clients, so she had to behave herself. But once we moved to the States, she had nothing else to do, so she became increasingly depressed. And my mother drinks to manage her feelings. It doesn't work, but she keeps trying.

A code of silence

Like I said, no one in my family spoke about my mother's drinking. This began with my father in France and continued with my grandmother in the States. Although my grandfather (her husband) was an alcoholic, she never admitted it. In fact, I've even heard her say that he never drank, which is completely delusional. Sure, my grandfather wasn't a complete wreck—he had a job and a social life—but he was undeniably an alcoholic. While he was still alive, my grandmother developed a habit of going to bed early so she wouldn't have to see him drunk. That was her coping mechanism during her marriage, and it later became her way of avoiding my mother's nighttime drunkenness.

I remember my grandmother once asked my brother and me, "Does your mother have another glass of wine after I go to bed?" And it was such a funny thing to ask, because Mom actually got drunk on vodka most of the time, not wine. But I guess that was her way of delicately approaching the subject without really touching it. And that's the closest anyone ever really came to discussing it. Even then, I remember feeling such a rush of shame at the question—as though *I'd* been caught drinking. I felt exposed and red-handed. I didn't perceive it as Grandma's way of trying to help. For her part, my mother was never able to admit that she was drunk. She was always just "very tired."

Coming out

Despite everything, my mother and I have always spent a lot of time together, and often enjoy each other's company. And yet she was the very last person I told I was gay. I think this is because I had decided that if she didn't have to talk about her drinking, I didn't have to talk about my sexuality. I thought maybe if I didn't bring up her slurred speech and emotional breakdowns, I didn't have to tell her I was attracted to men. And even when I finally did come out to her—because I'd already told everyone else— we hardly talked about it. She didn't have any kind of response at all, really.

It could have been worse, I suppose. When I came out to my father (who was still in France) he clung to the belief that homosexuality was a phase I'd grow out of. And when it became clear it wasn't, our already rocky relationship deteriorated quickly. In a way, though, my mother's silence was equally upsetting, because it was another example of how we never talk about difficult things.

Selective memory

When she couldn't simply avoid talking about something, my mother would often claim to have forgotten it. She would sometimes make irrational demands and then act surprised when I confronted her about them later. While my brother and I were in high school, we never really had a curfew, but one night when I was going out, my mother randomly decided I had to be home at eleven p.m. I was seventeen at the time and it was just absurd. We had a forty-five-minute argument about it, and I was so mad at her. But the next day, when I brought it up, she said, "Oh, I would never have said eleven. I must have meant one o'clock!" And I said, "We talked about it for forty-five minutes!" But she claimed not to remember any of it.

....

Research shows that heavy alcohol use can damage memory, sometimes permanently. Many people will not fully remember events or conversations that occurred while they were drunk.

....

How I coped

As a young child, I wasn't very good at coping. I assumed that my mother was drinking because I had done something wrong. When I got to high school and finally understood that my mom was an alcoholic and it wasn't my fault, I started acting out. I sometimes did this academically, probably because I knew that was important to her.

By the time I was sixteen or seventeen, I was very depressed and I let my normally high grades start to slip. I became a terrible procrastinator and couldn't bring myself to finish anything. I think this was partly my way of retaliating for everything, but partly I was just so depressed I couldn't do well even if I tried. Fortunately, when I did perform, I made up for the times when I wasn't performing, so I still managed to graduate at the top of my class.

Learning to talk about it

With time, I learned to cope in more effective ways. And ultimately, I learned to talk about my mother's alcoholism. It took a long time for talking to be helpful, though. At first, I confided in Thérèse. The two of us kept in touch after I left France, but we always used very pointed, hurtful language to talk about our mothers' habits. We called them drunks and other unkind names.

Later, in high school, I spoke with a school therapist about my mother's drinking. And I think that was the first time I talked about it in a way that wasn't as poisonous. But I was definitely still coming from a place of anger. And of course, being gay added a whole other layer of complexity to my teenage years. So it was a very isolating time. The only people I was able to talk to were outsiders, and I could only talk to them in a sarcastic, dismissive way. To this day, even my twin brother and I have never really spoken about my mother's drinking. I think this was because we grew up surrounded by walls of silence, and speaking became threatening to us.

Where it has left me

It's hard for me to look back and say my mother's drinking did "x," but it continues to be very difficult for me to talk about my feelings. I also live with a terrible fear of people changing. I assume that if someone says anything positive to me, they're either lying or they'll soon change their minds. I can't bring myself to believe nice things, unless they're repeated over and over again … especially when it comes to love and affection.

Emotions also scare me—particularly great displays of emotion like the ones my mother was prone to when she was drunk. I tend to blow ordinary interactions out of proportion and assume that, if someone raises their voice at me, we'll probably never speak again. For a long time, people crying made me very uncomfortable as well, but I'm slowly getting over some of these things.

My brother, Remy, is even worse. To this day, he's never been in a relationship. And as difficult as I find it to talk about my feelings, he's basically completely unable to do so. He has a tough time connecting with other human beings, something directly related, I think, to our experience as kids. My mom is still drinking, and it still upsets me. But now that I'm on my own, it's easier for me to avoid her when she's in really rough shape.

No judgment

About a year ago, I was taking the subway to work and there was a teenager on the platform with his mother. She was visibly very drunk and very poor. His situation was probably even worse than mine growing up, because my mother would never have been intoxicated in the middle of the day like that, and we were never broke. And you could tell that this boy was so embarrassed about the whole thing and that he thought everyone waiting for the subway was judging him.

I so badly wanted to tell him that no one was looking at him with judgment, and that he had no reason to be ashamed. I wanted to tell him that, if anything, people felt only great sympathy for him. I think that's what I missed out on, growing up: someone to tell me that I had nothing to be ashamed of. I wish I'd said something to him. Maybe next time I see something like that, I *will* speak up.

We Were Dealt the Same Hand

We Were Dealt the Same Hand

When Nicola and her brother, Kevin, were growing up, Kevin was hooked on the prescription painkiller OxyContin. Nicola's not sure why his addiction got so out of control, but she's proud that she turned out different.

Watching over me

My brother was always very overprotective. Our mom and dad got divorced when I was a year and a half old and he was three, and I'm pretty sure that he was trying to shield me from things even then.

We spent most of our time at Mom's, and I think he felt obligated to look out for me because Dad wasn't there. It became more obvious when we were older and he started taking drugs that made him paranoid. I think mostly he wanted to protect me from people like himself. He would worry about the places I went, the boys I dated, the people I hung out with. He would say things like, "Be careful," "You can never tell if someone's got a knife," and "Some people are crazy." It became a joke between my girlfriends and me, because a lot of them had older brothers around my older brother's age, but Kevin outdid them all. In a funny way, he was totally oblivious to it. He'd just say, "You're my sister," as if it was normal to be that over the top.

How it began

Kevin started drinking when we were still in elementary school, and by the time he was in ninth grade he was smoking cigarettes and pot too. I guess it was cool at the time, and a lot of his friends were doing the same thing. I wasn't dumb, I knew what he was doing. All throughout high school, he was part of the cool crowd—always smoking pot and drinking. We went to a Catholic high school in a small town, so I guess there wasn't much else to do. And the more he drank and smoked and used, the more overprotective he got.

From pot and booze to worse

The pot and the booze were just the beginning. Things got really bad after Kevin started experimenting with other drugs. He and his friends would carry around little folded-up pieces of colorful paper, each with a different drug inside—among them, OxyContin. It was this whole world that I wasn't a part of. For a while it seemed kind of fun and interesting, and I could see why Kevin would want to be a part of it. But I couldn't understand why he was never able to draw the line and acknowledge that his drug use was getting out of hand. He always had to have total control over my life, but he had no control over himself.

Many addicts, despite being unable to control their own dependencies, are very controlling of those around them. This is often a way for addicts to avoid being held accountable for their behavior.

Once, just after I got my driver's license, a friend of mine was having car troubles and I went to pick her up. I was just going to drive her home after the tow truck came to get her car, but Kevin got all crazy. He said to me, "Listen! Don't you get out of that car. You roll your window down and make her come to you. It's not safe to be walking around on the side of the highway." He was so stressed out about it that I'm pretty sure he followed me in his car to make sure I did what he said.

Hardly ever home

I'm pretty sure Kevin first got Oxy from a guy that my mom was dating at the time. And after he started taking it, he was hardly ever around. If you asked him where he was going, he would just say, "Out." And when he *was* home, he was always sleeping or cranky. Of all the different drugs he took, nothing compares to the way

OxyContin affected him. It turned him into a totally different person. He could sometimes be an asshole even when he wasn't on drugs, but Kevin after he started taking OxyContin was ten times the usual amount of asshole. Out of nowhere, he would yell and throw fits. It was terrible. Terrifying. He was not my brother—he was a monster. When he couldn't manipulate people to get his way, he would become furious with them. The personality switch was as immediate as turning on a lightbulb. He had my mom and me walking on eggshells all the time.

··

When people abuse OxyContin, they will often experience mood swings and become agitated or aggressive. This is because OxyContin affects brain chemistry, and can lead to long-term problems regulating emotions.

··

Whatever it took

Kevin told outrageous lies and did anything and everything to get his hands on drug money. He would steal prescription pads from doctors' offices and fill them out himself, or he would break into cars and sell anything he found inside. Once, he even had a gun in our house. I don't know where he got it, but it sure scared me.

At the time, our mom was thinking of buying a car from one of our neighbors and she went over to his house to talk to him about it. The guy was married, but he tried to kiss her and insinuated that he would give her a good deal for the car if she had sex with him. Mom made the mistake of telling Kevin about this. You should have seen him. "He's done," Kevin said. "This guy is finished. I'm going to blow his fucking kneecaps out." We managed to talk him down, but I was always afraid that he would do something really crazy one day.

Kevin was angriest of all when he was in between doses. See, OxyContin is a painkiller, so when you use it a lot, it decreases your ability to handle pain without it. I tried it once myself. I wanted to see what had turned my brother into this totally different person. It was awful. I couldn't sleep while I was on it, and I felt really itchy. After the high wore off, it was even worse. For three days, I had sore muscles and bones all over. I couldn't imagine why you'd ever want to take it a second time—except maybe to make the soreness go away.

My parents ignored it

Mom and Dad never really did anything about Kevin's drug use. Dad was a really straitlaced guy, and every now and then he'd try to put a stop to it, but he didn't take it that seriously. He was very naive about my brother. For the longest time he believed Kevin when he said he wasn't smoking cigarettes, even though there were yellow stains on his fingers. During high school, Kevin wasn't even trying to hide things. He would leave empty bottles lying around his room and would yell at Mom. And still our parents never really did anything about it.

Every now and then, Mom would say, "That's it. You're going to live with your father." Dad was way less of a pushover. He would come and take the TV out of his room and throw away all of his beer bottles. But when push came to shove, Mom would usually change her mind. Kevin sometimes threatened to leave home altogether if he was forced to live with Dad. I think Mom was afraid he'd follow through and she'd lose her baby. I guess I understand that, but I think sometimes her emotions got in the way of what needed to be done.

I think in a lot of ways Mom was just too scared of Kevin. She was terrified of drugs too. She had a really strict father growing up, and she had always been taught that you could end up dead if you took drugs. Either that or you'd get busted and end up in jail. So my mom was more worried about the fact that drugs were dangerous and illegal than about the fact that they were ruining Kevin's life.

Dad's other family

When I was in tenth grade, our dad built a nice house with his new wife. She had kids too and raised them very differently. They were allowed to take the bus into the city at a really young age and they got huge allowances compared to us. Not to mention, my dad's wife was spending a lot of our family's money. Meanwhile, Kevin and I didn't get anything. So as you can imagine, that didn't sit well with him. He got this notion into his head that one day Dad was going to die and his new wife would take all his inheritance. He became really obsessed with that idea. To be honest, I was kind of annoyed too, but never to the same degree as Kevin.

For a while, Kevin and I did move in with Dad and his new family. Kevin was going to have the big room over the garage where the pool table was; he just had to quit smoking. (By then our dad had accepted that he was addicted to cigarettes.) But he couldn't do it and so he ended up back at Mom's, where no one told him what to do.

How I coped

When it came to Kevin, I would usually keep my mouth shut. I knew there was no point in arguing with him. Sometimes I would try to get information out of him about where he was going or what his plans were, but it rarely worked. But I was always so eager to know anything and everything that he was willing to tell me, however small. It felt like he had so many secrets, and I wanted to know what they were. But most of them were pretty ugly,

I think. It's funny, though: he was so private about his own life but demanded to know everything about mine.

Even though Kevin did his best to protect me from everything (including himself) I think I matured quickly. I remember thinking about really weird things when I was still very young. I would sit in the playground wondering: *What would the world be like if I wasn't here? Where would I be if I wasn't in my body?* And I would always come back to the same answer: it wouldn't matter. None of us matter, really. That was before Kevin started taking drugs all the time. But I kept having those kinds of thoughts as I got older, and I think it was because of everything I was exposed to.

The silver lining was that nobody ever gave me shit for anything because of Kevin. When I was getting to the age where I was hanging out with him and his friends, I had a big crush on his friend Tracy's boyfriend. Nothing ever really happened between us, but we used to hang out. And I guess he had told Tracy, because she was giving him a hard time, but she never said anything to me. She was always really nice to me, even though I was hanging around with her boyfriend. And I'm pretty sure it's because she knew that Kevin was looking out for me. So, thanks to Kevin, I never had to deal with any bullying or gossip from anyone.

Turning out different

What did upset me was the fact that things never got better for Kevin. When we were growing up, my best friend, Casey, had a brother the same age as Kevin. They lived right down the street and Kevin and Jeff always used to get high together. Only with Jeff, it was just a temporary thing. By the time high school was over, he had cleaned up his act and had been accepted to study chemical engineering. But Kevin never really got over it. Instead of studying anything, he ended up in jail and, later, rehab. So her brother and my brother were best friends growing up, but they landed in totally different places. There were other guys at our high school too, guys that were just like Kevin and did a lot of drugs for a while but eventually got their lives together.

That's something I don't really understand. Why didn't Kevin end up in a better place, like those guys? Why, for that matter, did Kevin do drugs when I didn't? We were more or less dealt the same hand of cards. We both had divorced parents and grew up in a boring town, but I always knew where to draw the line. Maybe I have Kevin to thank for that. I could always look at him and see what I didn't want to become—what I had to avoid. But he didn't really have anyone to look to or see as an example in the same way. I always had him looking out for me and protecting my reputation, so I was never afraid to walk away from a situation that made me feel uncomfortable. He, on the other hand, never backed down from any challenge. So I sometimes feel proud that I turned out differently, but I wish I could say the same for Kevin.

Kevin, today

I don't see much of my brother these days since we're not living together anymore. Truth be told, I'm kind of afraid of running into him, because he's still so aggressive and angry. I've seen him around a few times and he's wasting away, almost to the point of being dead. I'm not sure if he's still using or not, but it sure looks that way. It's hard to see him that way, but it makes me want to avoid him. Like I said, he taught me how to steer clear of bad situations, and now I feel like that applies to steering clear of him.

Who's My Real Dad?

Who's My Real Dad?

Karl didn't know about his
dad's cocaine addiction
until, as part of his recovery,
his dad apologized for it.
For Karl, it was only after
"sorry" that the pieces
began to fall into place.

Finding out

Growing up, I never knew my dad was a cocaine addict. He hid it so well that my mom didn't even know for a while. And truth be told, we had a pretty normal life, for the most part.

> *Many addicts are amazingly good at hiding their dependencies from friends and family. They will do or say anything to keep their addiction from being discovered, and in some cases are not even aware of how deceptive they're being.*

When I was a kid, my dad would sometimes lecture me about not doing drugs. He'd say, "I experimented with plenty of different substances and it's a bad idea. Never do what I did." But it never occurred to me that he was *still* doing drugs. It wasn't until he started going to meetings of a group called Cocaine Addicts Anonymous that he decided to tell my brother and me about his addiction.

By that point I was seventeen, but when I look back I think I've always known something was up with my dad. I could never really put my finger on it, though.

As it turns out, he was doing cocaine pretty heavily beginning when I was eleven and going until I was at least thirteen. When he first told me that, I was more curious than scared or angry, because by then he had stopped and I didn't have much to be angry about. But it did make me wonder if cocaine was the reason he used to get so mad. Sometimes when I was younger, I would be crying or upset about something, and he would grab my arm to get me to stop or make me listen. And when he told me about his addiction, he apologized for this too. He says he did it because of the cocaine.

Dad's anger

I wasn't the only one who dealt with my dad's anger. A lot of my early childhood memories involve listening to my parents fight. Mainly it was my dad shouting. I hardly ever heard what it was about, but I sure heard the yelling. I would usually try to drown it out, or I'd just go to my room. Dad never hurt anyone in our family, and I'm pretty confident that he never hurt anyone in his life, but he sure did know how to argue. And if I ever pushed or hit him when I was little and upset, he would hit me back—never as hard as he could, but hard enough that I could feel it.

Other signs

He worked as a software engineer, and I used to hang out in his office all the time because it was close to our house. Usually I would sit outside his door, and sometimes, when I'd walk into his actual office, he would say, "No, no, no! You can't be in here right now. I'm doing important work." But after I left, I'd peek through the window beside his door and he would be sitting there doing nothing—just staring off into space. So I noticed lots of weird things like that. I never came to any conclusions about it, though. I never had any idea that he acted the way he did because of drugs. And it was so interesting when he told me that he was using, because suddenly I realized that maybe his actions would have been completely different if it weren't for cocaine; maybe the guy I grew up with was not my real father. So in that sense, it was a real shock to the system.

How it changed him

I can only assume the reason my dad started doing hard drugs in the first place was to help him deal with the stress of work, and life in an expensive city like San Francisco. It gave him energy and helped him get things done, so I guess, if it hadn't been for the cocaine, he wouldn't have been able to be as on top of things. But I'm pretty sure he also would've been less angry toward people. And he would have been healthier too. When I was a kid, I didn't sleep very well, and I'd wake up in the middle of the night all the time. But no matter what time of night I got up, my dad would still be awake. So that was another thing that sort of fell into place when he finally told me about his addiction.

The good thing about our shared sleeplessness was it usually meant that I got to see him a lot. But every now and then, instead of keeping him awake, the drugs would make him crash completely. That's the thing about cocaine: doing it gives you a jolt of energy and keeps you awake, but then afterward it can make you irritable and extremely tired. So all in all, I guess it helped him to get through work, but it also made him less active and more zoned out around us at times. I think that was just one of the ways it was bad for him. He made drugs a part of his daily routine and his body paid the price.

Sustained use of cocaine can cause heart problems and respiratory failure, as well as seizures and headaches. People who use cocaine for a long time can also develop a tolerance to its effects, meaning they have to take more each time in order to experience the same high.

Drinking too

When I was fourteen, we were pretty much forced out of the building we were living in and moved to a much tinier apartment. That was stressful for our family. At the time, I didn't think about my dad or realize that his expensive cocaine habit might have had something to do with it. I didn't even know he *had* a cocaine habit back then. But I *had* begun to notice his drinking. Sometimes I'd be sitting in the living room watching television and he'd come into the room, get a bottle of booze out of the liquor cabinet, and just do a shot. It was as though it was part of a normal day.

I'd say to him, "Why do you drink so much?"

And he'd say, "I'm not drinking that much. It's healthy for people to have a shot of alcohol every day."

"Okay," I'd say. "I guess I don't know much about it."

So I kind of accepted it. And even though I was aware of his drinking in a way that I wasn't aware of his cocaine use, I still didn't think about it that much. I certainly didn't think he was an alcoholic. It wasn't as though he walked around with a beer in his hand all the time. But it seemed to me that he relied on those shots. It was like he was dependent on booze, without ever being visibly drunk. And so drinking also became part of his normal day, without changing his behavior that much.

How I coped

It's hard to say how I coped with my dad's cocaine addiction as a kid because, like I said, I wasn't really aware of it. But when I was little, I was quiet and often played by myself. I watched a lot of television and was very into video games. Sometimes I would go to the park and hang out with friends, but I never spoke much. Looking back, that's kind of strange because both of my parents were very outgoing. It's not like they had no shame, but they certainly weren't quiet and they liked to socialize a lot.

One thing I think I did as a kid was bottle up my emotions. This meant that sometimes I would have angry outbursts where things came to the surface. It was usually small things that would prompt them, like not getting a toy or something. That's when my dad would grab my arm like I described earlier.

Still my dad

Even though all this was happening, I still just thought of my dad as my dad. I mean, he still taught me to play baseball and soccer and hockey, and most of the time he was fun to be around. So I never thought of him as bad, and life never seemed all that unusual. Sure, we were never the kind of family that had meetings or ate dinner together, but we still did fun stuff. The four of us would go visit relatives or friends out of town. And whenever we were on vacation together, we enjoyed each other's company. We could talk about almost anything. I knew I could come to my parents if I had major problems. But I never had major problems as a kid, or at least nothing I couldn't deal with myself. So my dad and I had a good relationship, despite his addiction.

Where things stand

In a way, there was more to cope with later on, when I finally found out about my dad's addiction. When he first told me about it, I wasn't sure what to say and was just kind of speechless. I never talked about it much with my mom or brother, because I think it affected us all in very different ways, and we've each dealt with it privately. But since coming clean, my dad has become a very different, very calm person. In a funny way, coming off drugs and going through therapy has made him more unfamiliar to me than drugs ever did. He's very obsessed with spirituality now, because of the support meetings that he goes to, and he can be a little pompous sometimes. I once told him that I had started drinking coffee, and he said, "You know that's an addiction, right?" It was like he was saying, "I'm an expert on addiction, so now I can lecture you about coffee." So in some ways, sobering up has changed him for the better, but in others it has also made him less real to me. He's so Zen and health focused that he's hardly anything like the dad I used to know.

Virtually all hard drugs cause personality changes. So coming off those drugs also causes the user's personality to change. To someone like Karl, who only ever knew his father as an addict, a sober parent can be a very unfamiliar one.

One of the ways that I've dealt with finding out about my dad's addiction is by supporting other people who are dealing with addiction issues. Whenever I have a friend who is having a problem with drugs, I tell them about my father's experience. I tell them that drugs are a crutch and that I've seen what they can do. I tell them that being a functioning addict isn't okay. After all, even though drugs don't seem to have changed my dad's behavior that much, I know they hurt his health. He sometimes slurs his speech or forgets words, and I think it's because the drugs damaged his brain. He used to joke about it, but he doesn't anymore. Now he says, "Shit. Why am I doing this?" And I know the time he spent doing drugs will affect him in the long run. So I guess this whole experience has made me more sensitive when it comes to drug problems, and has given me a feeling of responsibility to help anyone I can.

She Thought We Were Beautiful

Carmella's mom was
not only an alcoholic—
she was also bulimic. It didn't
take long for Carmella to
realize that sometimes your
only option is to walk away
from your parents …
even if you aren't ready.

Finding out

It wasn't because my mom was drunk that I found out about her alcoholism. I was too naïve to realize that booze was the reason she acted the way she did. Instead, I found out because I liked to borrow her clothes. She had this big walnut dresser and there was a drawer in it that was full of scarves. One time when I was about eleven, I was rooting through this drawer and found a huge, half-empty bottle of wine. But I didn't suddenly realize: *Oh! I'm the child of an alcoholic.*

At that point, my mom was still a high-functioning addict. She was not abusive, and she wasn't lying on the couch during the day or skipping work. But she had lots of self-esteem issues. She didn't think she was smart enough, or good enough, or successful enough. So my theory is she drank to escape feeling shitty about herself. And although she kept her drinking under control until I was ten or eleven, it eventually became impossible to ignore.

Many alcoholics suffer from low self-esteem, which often contributes to their decision to start drinking. Their feelings of worthlessness then make it even more difficult for them to deal with the addiction they've acquired.

Things changed

Something happened around the time I hit puberty that caused things to fall apart. I think it might have had to do with the fact that my mom had just finished a PhD. She wanted to be a successful scholar and it was a lot harder for her to do that than she had expected. So suddenly she found her career very disappointing, and all her other insecurities began to catch up with her.

Even then, my mom hardly drank in front of my younger brother, Graeme, or me. So when I started getting older and having friends whose parents would come home from work and pour themselves a Scotch, I thought that was so strange. I was confused by the fact that they didn't try to hide it, and by the knowledge that my mom had a problem and they didn't, necessarily—despite drinking so openly.

How it played out

Although my mom didn't drink in front of us, sometimes it *was* painfully easy to tell she'd been drinking. One weekend, for instance, she took Graeme and me up to a cottage that our family owned. We were actually having a fairly good time. But then one of my cousins showed up with his girlfriend. My extended family doesn't get along very well. I could tell my mom was unhappy that they were there, and I guess that made her drink.

Mom had the pullout bed in the living room and I was in the room next door. The evening after my cousin arrived, I woke up because I heard some really awful gagging noises. I discovered that Mom had made herself incredibly sick and was sitting on the floor trying to clean up her own vomit. I had to clean up the mess and help her back into bed.

It's really awful to feel disgusted by your own parent. I sometimes try to think about what it would be like if I had an abusive parent who punched me or hit me, and I assume then you'd feel powerless. But seeing them weak is the opposite: it makes you feel stronger than them, except you don't want to. It sounds terrible, but it's kind of like you want to put them out of their misery.

Trying to stay thin

It took me a while to realize that, in addition to being an alcoholic, my mother was bulimic. First, I began to notice that she had a lot of unusual rules around food. Whenever we'd go out for meals, she would get a salad. Once in a blue moon she would also get muffins for breakfast, but would only nibble around the edge. She took no pleasure in cooking, and only ever made Jell-O. My dad wasn't much of a cook either, so we had lots of TV dinners growing up.

Despite all this, it wasn't until I became bulimic too that I finally understood just how far my mom's disease went. I was fifteen when I started sneaking away from the table to throw up after dinner—and that's how I realized my mom had been doing the same thing for quite some time. We had two bathrooms in our house, and after a while it got so that my mom and I would each be in one of them puking, while my dad and brother sat at the table.

Dad didn't intervene

My dad never did or said anything about my mom's alcoholism, and he was the same with her bulimia. When I asked him about it later, he told me that he was terrified, and didn't know how to intervene. But he certainly knew what she was doing. And eventually they both knew that I was doing it too. They sent me to therapy for it when I was sixteen, and I hated it.

I didn't want to be there. I simply wasn't ready to stop throwing up. My mentality was: I'll stop when I'm really sexy and pretty. And on top of that, I thought it was so ironic because my mom had been in therapy for years and obviously it wasn't doing her any good.

How I coped

Despite sharing my mom's struggle with bulimia, I found her alcoholism repellent. I was very afraid of becoming like her in that way too, so I avoided her as much as I could. For the longest time I felt like the world had done bad things to me and that I didn't deserve them. I procrastinated a lot. I would do work I wasn't proud of, and then blame my circumstances. I was spoiling for a fight, and I liked feeling alone and neglected.

By the time I was thirteen, I desperately wanted to move out of my house. It took me years to understand that most thirteen-year-olds don't feel that way. They'll say, "Oh, I hate my parents, and they're no good, and I wanna leave," but they don't really mean it. I meant it. I wanted to go as soon as humanly possible. I spent my time fantasizing about having an apartment and paying bills. When I was sixteen, my parents split up. I couldn't bear the thought of being alone with my mom.

A place of my own

When I was seventeen, I told my mom that she was making me sick and blamed her for my eating disorder. I was convinced I had to go somewhere else where I would get better and not become crazy. So I got this really shitty one-room apartment with bright blue carpets and a shared kitchen in a pretty shady neighborhood. That lasted about two months, and then I moved in with a friend in an artist's loft with no walls—just one big room.

In some ways, living on my own was great because I'd wanted to do it for so long. But in other ways, it was a disaster. I was still dealing with an eating disorder and I didn't have a clue how to take care of myself. I would sneak back into my mom's house to eat things and throw them up. I was also drinking too much and messing around with drugs.

I think this was mostly because I was never taught how to do simple things like buy groceries and keep food in the fridge and have it not go bad. My parents never went grocery shopping or cooked or did anything like that, so I had no model to follow. I'd eat cake at the desserts café where I worked, or I'd buy seven zucchinis because they were on sale and then watch them all go bad. I remember one of my roommates once said, "What did your family eat? Didn't you watch them cook?" Laundry was the same. It would just appear on my bed, folded by my dad. I simply had no idea what to do, and my life deteriorated because of it.

Back with Dad

After about a year, I ended up moving back in with my dad. He was living in this tiny apartment above a fruit store. It was hard to see him like that, because we'd always been pretty well off while I was growing up. But my time there ended up being really good for me.

After years of doing next to nothing, my dad suddenly tried to help me with my eating disorder. At first, we went to a group therapy session for families of bulimic kids, and there were all of these parents there talking about how their daughters weighed eighty-nine pounds. And I remember my dad looking at me with raised eyebrows that said: *We don't need to do this for you, do we? You're not this bad, are you?* And I really wasn't, and we both knew it. So we left. Instead, he got me this great book that talked about how to overcome bulimia. I think he realized that I was too independent for group sessions; he knew I had to do it on my own. I read the book from cover to cover really fast and then started fighting. It happened slowly, one meal at a time. I began by keeping breakfast down … then lunch … and eventually, one day, dinner.

Bulimia affects everyone differently, and is hard to beat. For Carmella, it was easiest to fight the disease on her own. Some people find group therapy helpful. Bulimia can also cause health issues such as tooth decay, heart problems, and stomach ulcers, which may need treatment.

My dad did his best to treat me as an equal and didn't yell at me. It took him a while to come around, but I think he finally realized that trying to push me into anything wasn't going to work. So instead, he just gave me a place to get better. And a year later, when I wanted to move out on my own again, he didn't object. He believed me when I said I was ready—and that time, I really was.

No sympathy

My dad and I became a lot closer while I was getting over my bulimia, but I still didn't want to be around my mom. I just couldn't find it in me to try to understand her. I remember there was this really sad lady with no teeth named Eleanor who used to come by my work. She was pretty beat up and probably an addict herself, but I liked taking care of her. I'd give her free coffee and ice cream, and we'd sit around in this swanky café and talk.

One day my manager told me that I couldn't let Eleanor in anymore because she was "scaring away the other customers." She came by the next morning while he was there and I had to turn her away. She cried, and it was awful. For years afterward, I worried about her. Thinking back on it, it's strange that I had such sympathy for her but no compassion whatsoever for my own mom. I couldn't put her and my mom in the same category at all.

One time after I was living on my own again, I was Rollerblading home from work and I noticed this little car—a hatchback like my mom's—that had crashed into a traffic pole. As I was approaching it, I realized that it *was* my mom's car, and that she was standing outside it, crying.

I don't know if she was drunk at the time, but if not, she was probably hungover. And it was this really surreal moment where I had to decide: Do I keep going, or do I stop and comfort this lady? In the end I did stop, and I remember hugging her. I was taller than her on my Rollerblades, and I remember thinking: *I hate this. I hate being bigger, and stronger, and more capable than this woman who's supposed to be taking care of me!*

From bad to worse

After my parents' divorce was long over and I had moved out, my mom deteriorated even more. My dad started dating someone else and moved to another city to be with her. I think he had always felt so out of his depth with Mom that he was happy to get away. My brother had a room there and was welcome, but he didn't want to travel so far for school, so he ended up living in our old house, alone with my mom. She'd stopped doing any kind of maintenance on the place, so it was full of old wiring and aging appliances. Finally, there was a fire in the furnace one day.

The house was pretty badly damaged, and after that, my mom and brother were living in a long-term-stay hotel for a while. During that time, she lost control completely. I went to see them once while they were there, and she was wearing a robe and wandering around with a glass in her hand. Poor Graeme had to live through that while he was in high school. He said to me once, "You and Dad left me with her! That's what you did." He was right. I mean, he could have gone to live with my dad, but he was in a different city at that point. And I had long since moved out and wasn't prepared to be around my mom again. So we left Graeme with her.

How it affected me

As the child of an alcoholic, I always wanted my parents to address the problem—but the problem was *them*. And *they* were absolutely out of my control. I couldn't do anything about the fact that my mom was sick and my dad was helpless, and so I've spent the rest of my life feeling afraid of losing control. I'm very concerned about safety, and I don't open up to people very well.

It's hard for me to make connections with people. I'm very suspicious of outsiders, and I constantly feel like I'm about to be let down. When I do make a connection with someone, it's extremely hard for me to let go of him or her. When I was in my late twenties, my mom died of causes related to her years of drinking and bulimia. And it was very hard for me to have any relationships after that. Romantic relationships were especially tough, because I didn't want my emotions to be under someone else's control. But I'm learning that relationships don't have to be like that.

I went through a long period of time when I was very angry. I felt like a victim, and I thought that if my mom had loved me more, she would have stopped being an alcoholic. But a while ago, I came across a box of letters my mom had written to friends and family members over the years. I guess they had been returned to us after she died. They were full of these loving descriptions of the wonderful people that Graeme and I were turning into. And reading them was such a powerful experience for me, because I hadn't known that she thought we were beautiful. But now I know it's true.

Legal, but Not Okay

As an alcoholic, Brendan's mom was never actually breaking any laws or using any illegal substances. It took him a long time to realize that didn't make her actions okay.

My two moms

I often describe my mom as two totally separate people. One is the hardest-working woman I know: going back to grad school at the age of thirty-six, running a support program for teen moms, and leading the social-activist committee at our church. The other is a drunk.

My parents split up when I was six years old, and around that time it became clear to me that my mom had a drinking problem. She would pick me up after school and we would drive to the liquor store. Usually she'd buy one of those big bottles of wine that holds like eight normal glasses; most nights she'd drink the whole thing before she went to bed. But she still got up every morning, took me to school, went to work, and did her job. That really confused me. I think my parents' divorce had more to do with their relationship than her drinking, but the drinking certainly became worse after the split.

Basically, my mom was a textbook functioning alcoholic. She worked hard and always had a job, but after seven p.m. she became a whole different person.

> *A functioning alcoholic is someone who, despite their addiction, is able to lead a largely normal life. They can hold down a job and pay a mortgage, but they cannot prevent themselves from drinking routinely.*

When she got drunk, my mom was weirdly happy and disconnected. She would wander around the house and not pay any attention to what I was doing. She'd watch TV, or go into her room and close the door. She never seemed to have much of an appetite, which meant I had to fend for myself if I was hungry. She never asked me about school or wanted to see my report cards. Come to think of it, I don't think my mom has once checked to see whether I've done my homework or what I got on a test. And she certainly never made a habit of talking to me about my feelings—in particular, the fact that I was transgendered.

On my own

Drunk or sober, my mom has always been a very hands-off parent. In her view, as soon as I was old enough to read, I was old enough to keep myself occupied with books and games. She never arranged play dates or sent me to any extracurricular activities. That meant that I spent a lot of my time with adults rather than other kids. I don't think either of my parents has ever really enjoyed kids. I mean, they both loved me, but they worked hard to make me independent from a very young age. Things that other kids' parents did, like make their lunches, never happened in our family. Instead, I learned to cook when I was seven because I was worried that if my mom made dinner while she was drunk, something would catch fire.

I even had to fend for myself when I was sick. One time, shortly after my dad left us, I had a case of pediatric acid reflux so bad I missed a month of the third grade. I had no appetite and was experiencing chest pain all the time. And I have this very vivid memory of my mom being understanding and supportive during the day but then not caring at all at night. One evening I was lying on the couch in our living room, trying to explain to my mom that I was in a lot of pain, and she drunkenly threw a bottle of Pepto-Bismol at my head. I literally had to dodge it. She seemed to think I could just take a spoonful of this stuff and it would make me better. I was scared of her that night. I felt like she had violated the code of conduct that said it was her job to take care of me when I was sick. But alcohol did something to my mom that totally threw that code right out the window.

Being transgendered

We already had our challenges, but things were complicated further by the fact that I was transgendered: I was born in a girl's body, but I was really a boy. The nineties were a funny time for someone like me to grow up, because nobody knew much about being transgendered. Back then, child psychologists didn't really understand gender-bending kids like me. What I really needed was someone to help me sort out my confusion, but instead I had this neglectful mother.

I felt misunderstood. I *was* misunderstood. For a long time, I was scared of social situations, and my mom didn't help. She seemed to believe that my boyish tendencies were something I would grow out of. It wasn't until I was sixteen or so that she finally admitted: *Okay, this is not temporary. This is the deal.* But once she'd done that, it was like a done deal—nothing worth talking about. Her attitude became: *Of course you're transgendered. What's to discuss?*

Dad to the rescue

Between the ages of six (when my parents broke up) and thirteen, I only saw my dad one afternoon every week. I pretty much hated our get-togethers and didn't want anything to do with him. I felt like he was a deserter and had abandoned me with my mom, whom he knew was an alcoholic. His excuse was that he didn't want to put me through a custody battle. But my parents still get along, so this never made a lot of sense to me, because I'm not sure if there would have *been* a custody battle. I still have conversations with my dad where I say, "How could you do that to me? How could you leave me with her?" So for a long time, I was really mad at him and didn't want to see him, but when I was thirteen my mom said, "All right, you have to spend one night a week with your dad."

What was weird is that he ended up being helpful. Whereas my mom—in her drunkenness—kind of dismissed my whole experience of being transgendered, my dad sat down with me and listened. We spent many, many hours talking about it and he worked hard to understand it. By the time I was in high school, it was clear to me that my dad was more of an ally than my mom. My mom had made it clear that she wasn't all that interested in what was going on with me. Whether it was school or my being transgendered, she was too preoccupied—or too drunk—to pay attention. I still had to live with her, though.

How I coped

For the longest time, I was sure that my mom's drinking was my fault. I think that was partly because I went to a nice private school and we lived in a nice neighborhood and all the other kids I knew basically had perfect lives. They had two parents. They did nice things like go to ice skating lessons and play soccer. So I already felt like I must be doing something wrong because my single-parent family was so different from theirs. Plus there was the fact that I was transgendered, which also made us different.

••

Many addicts' children blame themselves for their parents' substance abuse. In the case of alcoholism, some children feel they are driving their parents to drink. In reality, the children of addicts are victims, and their parents' behavior is out of their control.

••

Above all I was certain that, if I talked to anyone about my mom's drinking, people would find out that we were even more different than we already seemed. So most of the people I grew up with had no idea that my mom was an alcoholic.

I think one of the ways that I dealt with the secret of my mom's drinking was by maintaining total academic control. Even though my mom didn't care how I did in school, it was essential to me that I get perfect grades and impress my teachers. I decided that if I couldn't control other parts of my life, I would control school.

I also took over many household responsibilities, so by the time I was seven I made all of our meals, bought a lot of the groceries, and even did some small repairs to broken fences and leaky faucets. On the one hand that was a burden, but on the other hand I found the responsibility comforting because it was something I could control.

Not breaking any laws

Growing up, I thought a lot about the fact that my mom wasn't doing anything illegal. Also, my mom would often tell me stories about people who were really over the edge. For a while she worked with drug addicts whose children had been taken away from them, so I knew that my situation wasn't as bad as theirs, and I felt like I didn't have all that much to complain about. I also believed that, if I spoke up, someone might take me away from my mom—like those addicts' kids—and no matter how bad things got, I didn't want that. So I thought my mom's drinking was just something that I had to deal with.

To make matters worse, a lot of liquor stores where I grew up were operated by the government, so I sometimes felt as though my mom's drinking was state sanctioned. I figured, if she's buying this booze from a store that's government run, how could it be wrong? On top of that, my mom was always trying to educate me about drugs and crime. She'd ask me questions like: *Where do drug deals take place?* And then in my head I'd compare that to: *Where do we buy alcohol?* And it's this nice, well-lit store with uniformed employees. So I think my mom sort of used that comparison to make me think that her behavior was somehow okay because it wasn't breaking any rules.

When things got ugly

By the time I was about fifteen, my mom had stopped drinking quite as regularly, partly because I'd confronted her about it once or twice. The drinking still happened, though, and in a way it just became less predictable. I was into acting at that point, and had just come home from a rehearsal one evening to find my mom passed out. Well, I accidentally woke her up and she was so angry that she chucked me against a dresser and tried to strangle me. By this point I was almost bigger than she was, and I was able to take her by the shoulders and lead her back to bed.

I still don't really understand what happened. I guess she was just so drunk that she was acting crazy, but that was an extremely scary moment. As soon as she fell back asleep, I ran to my room and sobbed hysterically for quite a while.

Another time, when I was about sixteen, my mom picked me up from my job at a grocery store near our house. I didn't have my driver's license yet, but she was clearly very drunk, so I had to drive. And I'm thinking, *Great—I got my learner's permit a month ago, I've never driven at night, and you're hammered!* So there I was, breaking the law because of her, and it just made me so angry.

When we finally got home and I was backing into our driveway, I was so mad that I deliberately backed the car into the side of our house. It was so totally unlike me. I rarely ever confronted my mom about her drinking, but for the next four years we had a huge scratch along the back of our car. It was done in retaliation, on purpose. And what was weird is she never got angry with me for it. She's never once said a word to me about it, or even acknowledged that it happened. It's the sort of thing that could have been repaired, but she never bothered.

Selective memory

Now, on the rare occasion that I find the courage to confront her about these events, my mother claims to have no recollection of them. She doesn't remember the night she tried to strangle me, or the incident with the car. There are a lot of things that she doesn't remember, or chooses to forget. And generally speaking, when I try to confront her about the bad times, there's one set of lines that she uses: "I still took you to museums. You still went to a great private school. You grew up in a church community. You have nothing to complain about." So her response whenever I try to talk to her about the stuff she's done is always: *Look at you. You're fine. No big deal.*

Where I ended up

My mom still drinks. I don't live at home anymore, but sometimes, when I call her in the evening, it's clear that she's plastered. She still only drinks after work, though, so my dad and I basically have an unspoken rule that we only call my mom's house if it's before seven p.m. Now that I'm older, my mom also tries to use me as an excuse to drink. She'll act as though she's buying a big bottle of wine so that we can share it. And meanwhile, she knows full well that I'm never going to have a drink with her.

Like I said, one of the benefits of my mom's drinking is that I did well in school. This was true in university as well. In my last year of university I broke a school record for academic achievement. What was funny is my mom came to my graduation ceremony and everyone was congratulating her and she had no idea what they were talking about; she didn't know why she "must be so proud." So, to this day, she's out of touch with what's going on in my life. For the most part that's okay, though, because what's going on in my life is pretty good, with or without her acknowledgment. And despite everything she did wrong, it's partly because her drinking forced me to become independent that I've been so successful.

I've Inherited the Good Stuff

I've Inherited the Good Stuff

When Mary-Rose was growing up, her parents—preoccupied with their addictions to work and alcohol—ignored her most of the time. It made her sad, but also turned her into a more resilient, independent person.

Me, alone

When I was little, I was alone a lot. My mom worked at an insurance company, and work was really important to her. She spent so much time in the office you could say she was a workaholic. My parents fought a lot and eventually split up when I was ten. After that, my mom ended up marrying her boss, and I think she felt like she had to work extra hard to prove that she wasn't just getting promotions because she was married to him. She also liked to have nice things, so it was important for her to make money so she could afford them. That made me mad sometimes, because I felt like expensive stuff was more important to her than I was. My dad, meanwhile, was an alcoholic, just like his dad was when he was a kid. As far back as I can remember, he drank a lot and would often come home late at night from the bar.

So that's me: Mary-Rose, sitting on the couch waiting for Mom to come home from work and Dad to come home from the bar. I look back and I see myself looking at the clock thinking, *Great, they're an hour late again*. We ate dinner late a lot, and I was always hungry. Sometimes it was so late that I would lose my appetite altogether. There was also the anxiety that came with not knowing what my dad would be like when he did come home. Sometimes he was angry when he was drunk, but sometimes he was affectionate too.

Embarrassed by Dad

I have a brother too, Erik. He's a lot younger than me, and when we were both little I helped to take care of him and would feed him his bottle in the mornings. But when we got a bit older, he was a lot less shy than I was. So while I was spending time at home alone, he was usually out with friends. But I was never very social, partly because I felt ashamed a lot of the time, so it was easier not to be with people. I knew from being in other families' homes that most parents didn't argue the way my parents did. And my dad acted in ways that embarrassed me a lot of the time. He was always the guy who got drunk at family gatherings, for instance.

I remember one time when I was in ninth grade and my dad was supposed to pick my friend Katy and me up from a school dance. It was a Friday night, and normally my dad drank on Friday nights, but this time he had promised not to. But when he showed up, I knew right away he'd broken his promise. So the whole ride home, I kept talking loud and fast so that my dad wouldn't open his mouth. I knew that if he did, Katy would smell his breath. I probably should have been worried that he would crash the car, but I was way more afraid that my friend would find out that my dad was a drunk. After that, I never went to a school dance again.

Ignored and neglected

My dad's drinking definitely got worse after my parents split up, but there were some bad times before then too. Once, I had to go to the doctor's because I had plantar warts on my feet. And anyone who has had plantar warts knows that they can be really, really painful. Mine were. And I had to have them burnt off, so it hurt to walk afterward. So there I was, sitting at the doctor's office waiting for my mom to pick me up, but she never came; she was so busy at work that she forgot. My dad didn't come either, and I ended up having to walk all the way home, balancing on the sides of my feet so that my soles wouldn't touch the ground because it hurt too much.

Affectionate drunk dad

The thing is, though, it wasn't always bad. Like I said, sometimes my dad was very affectionate and friendly when he was drunk. And in some ways, I never got as mad at him as I did at my mom. I think the reason I felt that way was because everybody knows that alcoholism is a bad thing, but a lot of people don't even realize worka-holism exists.

After all, a lot of people get addicted to alcohol, and supposedly they can't really help it. It's like a medical condition—out of your control. So I could sort of under-stand that someone would choose alcohol over me. But I couldn't understand why my mom would choose work over me.

> *There is no generally accepted medical definition of workaholism, but it undoubtedly exists. A workaholic is someone who is addicted to work, and this is very different from someone who simply "works hard." Workaholics will log an extraordinary number of hours, and will often put work ahead of every other commitment in their lives.*

Sometimes when my dad was drunk, he would talk to me like I was a grown-up. I know that probably isn't the best thing for a kid, but at the time I really liked it. It made me feel mature. He was a journalist, and he would come home from work and drink and tell me about his problems with his coworkers and ask me what I thought about big issues, things like the death penalty and abortion. It felt special to talk about those things with my dad.

He relied on me a lot too—especially when I was ten or eleven, around the time I started going back and forth between my parents' houses. He would ask me how to operate the washer and dryer, and how to cook rice, and things like that. I didn't always know the answer, because I was little, but I wanted to help him, so I always did my best to figure it out. Sometimes he would complain about money, and I would slip some of my allowance dollars back into the pocket of his jeans. I think I did all that stuff because I felt like I was helping my dad to be less depressed and sad about the fact that my mom had left him. I even read over some of his articles for him, which also made me feel special and grown-up.

So that was the affectionate drunk dad. He was the one who would talk to me and look to me for help.

Angry drunk dad

Then there was the angry drunk dad. He was the one who locked my cat out of the house once when it was raining, when I was eleven. That was shortly after my parents split up, and my dad was feeling argumentative and depressed a lot of the time. I loved Cissy and used to take pictures of her and draw hearts around the frames. So she was outside meowing in the rain, but my dad wouldn't allow me to let her in. After that, I took my pictures of Cissy to all our neighbors' doors to ask if they'd seen her, but she never turned up. And the saddest part is it made perfect sense to me that the cat would leave. Because if my father would rather be drinking than spending time with me, and my mother would rather be at work than spending time with me, of course Cissy would rather be somewhere other than with me. It was a super, super sad time in my life, and I cried a lot over the next few weeks. By then my mother had gotten married to her boss, and I remember him saying to her, "You have to do something about this. She's depressed. She shouldn't be eleven years old and depressed."

Sometimes it's better to be ignored

My mom didn't help matters, though. She wasn't very nurturing and didn't appreciate how sensitive I was. I remember a time, shortly after Cissy went missing, that my mom and I were out shopping together. I was in such a good mood that I said to her, "Nothing could ruin this mood!"

"I bet I could ruin it with one word," she said.

Sure enough, she only had to say one word: *Cissy.* I just cried my eyes out after that. That was uncharacteristically mean of my mom, though. If anything, she just ignored me most of the time.

How I coped

As you can probably imagine, it was really important to me that my parents notice me. I tried hard to win their love and attention by being good. I couldn't wait for report card day, because I'd have this piece of paper that would prove to them what a fantastic job I was doing. I was usually disappointed, though, because they would just say, "Good job, Mary-Rose, another great report card." They were never as surprised or pleased as I wanted them to be. So I tried other things instead. I volunteered everywhere. I did bookkeeping at my church when I was just fourteen. I organized clothing drives for orphanages in China. I was part of every walkathon and coin drive— you name it!

My brother was different. He tried to get our parents to notice him by acting out. He experimented with drugs and drinking and became really belligerent. He was always getting into trouble from a really young age—and still is.

How it helped me

No matter what my brother or I did, neither of our parents ever really paid attention to us. They were both too busy with their addictions to work and booze. But the thing is, all this stuff made me stronger in some ways. Even though my parents didn't always notice it, I did really well in school and became very well-educated. Ever since I was little, teachers have liked me.

Because I worked so hard in school, I got into an excellent university, and was able to start my own business. And as a teenager I had the guts to go on all sorts of great adventures. I went to India and taught English in a women's shelter there. I went to Europe and saw famous works of art. I was able to do all that because I had to take care of myself when I was little, and those were amazing experiences for me. But it's still really important to me that people understand that I love my parents, despite the things they did wrong.

I recently went out for lunch with my dad and he told me that the thing he regrets most in life is that his marriage to my mom ended and the family was broken. He continues to drink and he'll sometimes call me when he's been drinking, but we have a pretty good relationship now. I still feel closer to him than I do to my mom. Interestingly, my mother has also acquired a fondness for wine in her later years, and will drink too much and say hurtful things like she used to. There's part of me that's afraid I could somehow become her without meaning to. I think that's why I have yet to have kids of my own. But I think mostly I've inherited the good stuff from her: the confidence and professionalism and determination.

Common Questions

Dr. Dennis Kimberley is a professor of social work at Memorial University, where he teaches courses on addictions treatment, child abuse, and human growth and development. He has more than forty years of experience in addiction therapy and child protection.

Q: I have a family member who sometimes behaves like some of the people described in this book, but I'm not sure if (s)he is an addict. How can I tell?

A: One of the first signs of addiction is that a family member is not taking on the roles and responsibilities that are expected of him or her given his or her age, stage, and situation. Instead, other family members—sometimes kids as young as four—are taking on those jobs. So if you find yourself performing tasks (like grocery shopping or cooking) that adults are performing in other households, addiction may have something to do with it. Sometimes, this gets to a point where a child is actually looking after the parent! That's called "parentification."

Anger, aggression, or withdrawal can also be signs of addiction. For instance, if a family member gets angry with you when tasks aren't completed, or blames you for their problems, addiction may be a contributing factor. Many addicts end up resenting their family members for completing the tasks they should be responsible for. So on the one hand, addicts often force their kids to take on more responsibility, but on the other hand, they don't like feeling as though their children are more powerful than they are.

Finally, addiction often leads to changes in a family member's ability to function outside the home. Addicts may behave strangely at work, in the community, or at social functions. This will often make those around them feel scared or embarrassed.

Q: Is my parent's addiction my fault?

A: It's very common for children to feel as though a parent's addiction has something to do with them. This is especially true of children who feel they are somehow unusual or high-maintenance. And even if they don't feel responsible for causing their parent's addiction, they may feel responsible for failing to make it go away. So feelings of guilt are not unusual, but that doesn't make them justified. Your parent's addiction is not your fault. Parents are the adults; it's their job to take care of you, not vice versa. It's their job—not yours—to make responsible decisions for themselves, you, and the family.

Q: Why are only some types of addiction against the law?

A: There is no simple answer to this question, and it's something that the people in charge of making laws are always grappling with. Part of the reason not every addictive substance is illegal is because it would cost too much money to prevent them all from being sold. Keeping illegal drugs off the streets is a very expensive thing for governments to do … and the more illegal drugs there are, the more it costs. Another reason some drugs aren't illegal is because governments want to be able to control the way they're distributed. For example, if cough syrup were against the law, some people might be more likely to use it in unsafe ways just for the thrill. But because it's legal, and sold in pharmacies, people are more likely to read the label and ask a doctor how to use it safely.

Q: Sometimes my family member is scary and violent when (s)he's drunk. What should I do when this happens?

A: If your parent (or any other family member) ever makes you feel unsafe, get help. Go and talk to somebody you trust to look out for you (like a grandparent) or contact your local child protection services (through a kids' help line). You might also feel comfortable talking to a teacher or a family friend. Extended family members may try to bury the problem or hide it. If you find this happening, it may be better to go to someone outside your family for help. Whatever you do, don't try to manage your family member's aggression on your own. You're likely to put yourself in danger. And don't be surprised if witnessing your family member's aggression leaves a mark on you. Studies have shown that even if you're not the victim of aggression, seeing violence happen can be very damaging. For some people, experiencing or observing violence can lead to nightmares, sleeplessness, feeling numb and disconnected, or living your life as if you're always on high alert. If this sounds familiar to you, again, seek help. Find an adult you trust to talk to.

Q: Sometimes, I just want to leave my family. But where can I go?

A: The answer to this question depends on your circumstances. If you're still a minor, your local child protection service will help you find somewhere to go. Oftentimes, they'll find you a home with another family member— an aunt, uncle, or grandparent. But if that's not a safe arrangement, they'll find you somewhere else to stay.

If you're older, but not yet ready to live completely on your own or support yourself, there are programs designed to help you too. Generally called youth services programs, they can be found in most regions, and are usually aimed at those who are sixteen and older. Youth services typically work at finding housing and work for their clients, and may be able to arrange educational supports. Please do everything you can to access the help provided by these programs before leaving home. Generally speaking, kids who head out on their own without some kind of safety net in place don't do very well.

Q: How common is it for the children of addicts to become addicts? I'm worried it might happen to me.

A: Statistically speaking, the children of addicts have a much higher chance of becoming addicts than the average person. But knowing that can go a long way. If you're worried about becoming an addict, treat drugs, alcohol, and addictive behaviors (for example, gambling, gaming, and social networking) with great care. Think of addiction in the same way that people think of conditions like diabetes. If you come from a family where diabetes is really common, you may learn to eat less junk food and watch your weight to stay healthy. So if you come from a family where addiction is really common, why not steer clear of things that have the potential to be addictive?

Q: What will people think of us if my family member's addiction is discovered?

A: Chances are, no one's opinion of you will change all that much. If anything, you're much more likely to be greeted with sympathy and support than with ridicule or judgment. We live in a society where a growing number of people are likely to say, "That's good to know, how can I help you?" The first step to getting that help lies in getting the words out over your lips to someone you trust. The longer you remain silent, the harder it may be to speak up when someone asks you the difficult question, "What's going on with you and your family?" Generally speaking, you can't begin healing until you've told someone about your family member's addiction. So the earlier you spill the beans, the sooner that healing process can start. If the first person you tell doesn't handle the news in the way you'd like, don't let that stop you from trying again. Soon, you'll tell someone who will be supportive of you.

Q: I want to speak up about my family member's addiction, but I'm afraid that if I do, he or she will be punished or separated from me. How can I avoid this?

A: The likelihood of a parent or family member going to jail or being punished in any significant way is very slim. So too is the likelihood of you being removed or separated from your family. Child protection people do not swoop into homes and immediately take children away from their parents unless the situation is very, very bad. In most cases, an addicted family member will be given time, help, and a chance to overcome the addiction. The other thing to consider is that if things do escalate to a point where you are somehow separated from your family, there's a very real chance that it is for the best. In many cases, once children are living somewhere safe (whether that's with another family member or in foster care) they say they are relieved to be there. It can be hard to leave your family, and it may make you feel disloyal, but you have to take care of yourself and surround yourself with people who care for you in a healthy way.

Q: Sometimes I feel like I'm the only one who has an addicted family member. How common is addiction in families?

A: There are many different estimates, and it depends what you consider addiction, but I would say that addiction affects a minimum of one in five families. That's huge. That means a lot of the people you know probably come from families dealing with some kind of addiction. That could be a parent, sibling, aunt, or uncle. It could be alcohol, street drugs, prescription drugs, gambling, social networking, gaming, or sex. But at least twenty percent of all families are affected by some type of substance use/abuse, or a non-chemical addiction. Your family is not the only one.

Q: How do behavioral addictions to things like gambling or work differ from substance addictions?

A: Behavioral addictions are more similar to substance addictions than not. While it's not a perfect match, if somebody's addicted to gambling or video games, some of the same things are happening inside their bodies that are happening to people who are addicted to alcohol or heroin. Addicts' brains, moods, and relationships are affected in very similar ways whether they're addicted to something they consume or something they do. So while there are some differences between substance addictions and behavioral addictions, the two are very close, with each having similar impacts on family members.

Q: I feel ready to confront my family member about his/her addiction. How should I do this?

A: The most important thing to consider when you feel you've reached a point where you're ready to confront your addicted family member is to decide whether you should be doing it alone. In my opinion, it's almost always best to have at least one buddy. Better still, get a group of appropriately supportive people together. Confronting someone alone can be difficult, because you start to second-guess yourself and addicted people are often masters at dodging blame. If you're with at least one other person who feels the same way you do, it becomes a lot easier to say, "that's not true," or "stop denying it," or "give it up." I worked with one girl who was about twelve years old when she confronted her mom about her addiction. She took the lead in doing so, but she also had a few adults there to back her up, which I think was very, very important.

Q: I often feel like I don't belong—at home, at school, or anywhere. Is this normal?

A: Many people who grow up with an addict in their household feel this way. Even when they are at home with family or at school with friends, they feel like an outsider. They report feeling alone and lonely in the presence of others. And while this is a perfectly normal way to feel, it can be very difficult and isolating. It can also mean that you get into a situation where you're inclined to leave home without a safety net in place. So if you find yourself feeling this way, it's really important that you do what you can to seek out people who make you feel more connected—in healthy ways. Those people might be extended family members, or they might be your friends' parents and siblings. Whoever they are, it's okay for you to say to them, "Can I come stay with you for a while until I sort this out?" Gradually, you'll start to feel like you belong and are connected again.

Q: How can I move on?

A: As the child of an addicted person you are not responsible for your family member's addiction. Nor is it your job to cover for him or her. If you allow yourself not to feel a sense of responsibility, you'll have more energy to heal and get on with your life in a healthy way. Remember, you can't control your parent's addiction, but with the support of others who are capable, safe, and looking out for your interests, you can gradually take more control of your feelings, actions, well-being, relationships, and future. To do that, you'll need the energy and care you might normally put into managing your addicted family member's needs. You are important. Your needs are important. Your future in your best interest starts now.

For Advice and Help

This section lists only a small sample of the many resources available to help you. Your school counselor, local library, or church may also be able to help you find information, resources, and support. You may also refer to the question and answer section on page 108.

In an emergency ...

If you're in the United States, there are many excellent crisis lines that you can call 24/7. You can use the Internet to find one in your area by googling your location + "crisis line," or you can always call 1-800-442-HOPE or 1-800-273-TALK from anywhere in the U.S. These are two confidential, toll-free hotlines for people experiencing any kind of emotional distress.

If you're in Canada, you can always call Kids Help Phone, at 1-800-668-6868 or visit www.kidshelpphone.ca to chat with someone online. They're a totally anonymous source of information and can communicate in both English and French. They can provide you with immediate access to trained counselors, and help you explore your options.

In an emergency, never be afraid to phone the police. They will always do their best to help you, even if you or a family member has done something illegal.

For someone to talk to ...

If there's no emergency, but you are looking for more long-term support, there are a number of things you can try. Talk to another relative or if that's not an option try speaking with a teacher you like, or a school guidance counselor. Chances are, they can point you in the right direction. Don't be embarrassed or afraid to reach out for help.

There are also places online where you can connect with other young people who have addicted family members. A good example is www.coap.org.uk, which is the online home of a group called Children of Addicted Parents & People. They have discussion forums where you're free to post questions and comments anonymously, and have people respond to them.

If you're interested in joining a support group, consider finding an Al-Anon or Alateen chapter in your neigborhood. Al-Anon is an international fellowship of people whose lives have been affected by the alcoholism (and in some cases, drug abuse) of their loved ones. Find out more at www.al-anon.alateen.org.

For more information on addiction ...

If you're just looking for information, there are lots of good resources online. Some of these are specific to certain types of addiction but others contain general information on a variety of addictions.

There's the National Institute on Drug Abuse, which is based in the United States. Their website is: www.drugabuse.gov. The online home of the Centre for Addiction and Mental Health, an addictions research facility based in Canada, is www.camh.net. You can find great information there on all forms of addiction, as well as resources geared specifically toward children and teenagers.

The National Council on Alcoholism and Drug Dependence is another great resource. If you visit www.ncadd.org, you'll find information on a whole bunch of different types of addiction, as well as guidance on how to deal with drug, alcohol, and behavioral dependencies.

For treatment ...

If you are struggling with addiction, you're not alone. Children of addicts often find it harder to avoid developing dependencies of their own. But there are many places you can go for help. In the U.S., you can call 1-800-928-9139 for information on rehab centers in your area. Hazelden treatment centers can also be found across the United States, and can be reached toll-free at 1-800-257-7810 any day, any time. Their main website is www.hazelden.org.

There is even a Hazelden facility in Plymouth, Minnesota, specifically for teens and young adults, and their hotline is at 1-800-257-7800.

In Canada, some hospitals (such as the Hospital for Sick Children in Toronto) offer outpatient counseling for people between the ages of eight and seventeen who are struggling with substance abuse. Their number is 416-813-5097. Other similar programs exist across the country and can be found online.

For more information on treatment, you can always talk to your doctor, or visit a walk-in clinic in your area.